My friends—

Twenty-eight History
Making Speeches

by

Franklin Delano Roosevelt

Edited by
Edward H. Kavinoky *and* Julian Park

FOSTER & STEWART PUBLISHING CORP.
Buffalo, N. Y.

EDWARD H. KAVINOKY is a prominent Buffalo lawyer. He is a civic minded American citizen. He is past president of the Buffalo Council of Social Agencies and a spirited effective worker in local and national organizations whose sole purpose for existence lies in their unrelenting efforts to better the lot of mankind. He is a director of Foster & Stewart Publishing Corp.

JULIAN PARK is a distinguished educator. He is Dean of the College of Arts and Sciences of the University of Buffalo, Acting Librarian of the Grosvenor Library and one of those able citizens of a community who place at the disposal of their neighbors a deep cultural background and training combined with an acute, forward looking political sense.

PUBLISHERS' FOREWORD

We proudly present to the American people a chapter of our history, which began on March 4, 1933 and ended on April 12, 1945—a history written in the present tense by one who contributed most to its making—written like the score of a mighty symphony to be played directly to the ears and hearts of his countrymen.

Literally F. D. R. was the Voice of America—and what a voice! When we read these speeches we can hear again his vibrant living words. We were indeed a fortunate generation—for with the turn of a dial we could bring his shining magic into our homes and to get a little better insight and understanding of the events that were tumbling all about us.

For those who read this book in the future and who never heard his voice, it will not bring back the ringing, smiling tones, but it will at least evoke the substance of an era.

Years hence when radio will have been long supplanted by three-dimensional television these speeches will stand as a great landmark of the Golden Age of Radio and it will be a long time before their material will be improved.

When the proper Washington memorial is some day erected for Franklin Delano Roosevelt to stand with those of his great predecessors, we feel certain that its walls will be inscribed with excerpts from these speeches which will take their proper place alongside The Gettysburg Address and The Declaration of Independence, in the literary history of America.

The Publishers.

First Printing, September, 1945

Second Printing, November, 1945

TABLE OF CONTENTS

	Page
First Inaugural Address *March 4, 1933*	1
First Fireside Chat *March 12, 1933*	6
Second Fireside Chat *May 7, 1933*	10
Third Fireside Chat *July 24, 1933*	17
Address to the Federal Council of Churches "The Right to a More Abundant Life" *December 6, 1933*	24
Fourth Fireside Chat *June 28, 1934*	27
Second Inaugural Address *January 20, 1937*	33
Message to Congress *May 24, 1937*	38
Quarantine Address at Chicago *October 5, 1937*	42
Message to Congress *November 15, 1937*	47
Address at Thousand Island Bridge *August 18, 1938*	55
Talk at Queen's University *August 18, 1938*	59
Address at Charlottesville "The Dagger in the Back" *June 10, 1940*	62
Call for Full Response on Defense *December 29, 1940*	67

Message to Congress 76
January 6, 1941

Third Inaugural Address 84
January 20, 1941

Speech on German Submarine Attacks . . . 88
September 11, 1941

Speech on Pearl Harbor 95
December 9, 1941

Message to Congress on Relations with Japan . . 102
December 15, 1941

Message to Congress 113
January 6, 1942

Address on 60th Birthday 121
January 30, 1942

Broadcast on Washington's Birthday 123
February 22, 1942

Flag Day Address 132
June 13, 1942

New Deal Speech Before the Democratic National Convention 134
July 2, 1932

War Message to Congress 145
December 8, 1941

Response to Address by President Avila Camacho . . 147
April 20, 1943

Fourth Inaugural Address 150
January 20, 1945

Undelivered Address 152
April 13, 1945

FIRST INAUGURAL ADDRESS
March 4, 1933

I am certain that my fellow Americans expect that on my induction into the Presidency I will address them with a candor and a decision which the present situation of our Nation impels. This is preëminently the time to speak the truth, the whole truth, frankly and boldly. Nor need we shrink from honestly facing conditions in our country today. This great Nation will endure as it has endured, will revive and will prosper. So, first of all, let me assert my firm belief that the only thing we have to fear is fear itself—nameless, unreasoning, unjustified terror which paralyzes needed efforts to convert retreat into advance. In every dark hour of our national life a leadership of frankness and vigor has met with that understanding and support of the people themselves which is essential to victory. I am convinced that you will again give that support to leadership in these critical days.

In such a spirit on my part and on yours we face our common difficulties. They concern, thank God, only material things. Values have shrunken to fantastic levels; taxes have risen; our ability to pay has fallen; government of all kinds is faced by serious curtailment of income; the means of exchange are frozen in the currents of trade; the withered leaves of industrial enterprise lie on every side; farmers find no markets for their produce; the savings of many years in thousands of families are gone.

More important, a host of unemployed citizens face the grim problem of existence, and an equally great number toil with little return. Only a foolish optimist can deny the dark realities of the moment.

Yet our distress comes from no failure of substance. We are stricken by no plague of locusts. Compared with the perils which our forefathers conquered because they believed and were not afraid, we have still much to be thankful for. Nature still offers her bounty and human efforts have multiplied it. Plenty is at our doorstep, but a generous use of it languishes in the very sight of the supply. Primarily this is because rules of the exchange of mankind's goods have failed through their own stubbornness and their own incompetence, have admitted their failure, and have abdicated. Practices of the unscrupulous money changers stand indicted in the court of public opinion, rejected by the hearts and minds of men.

True they have tried, but their efforts have been cast in the pattern of an outworn tradition. Faced by failure of credit they have proposed only the lending of more money. Stripped of the lure of profit by which to induce our people to follow their false leadership, they have resorted to exhortations, pleading tearfully for restored confidence. They know only the rules of a generation of self-seekers. They have no vision, and when there is no vision the people perish.

The money changers have fled from their high seats in the temple of our civilization. We may now restore that temple to the ancient truths. The measure of the restoration lies in the extent to which we apply social values more noble than mere monetary profit.

Happiness lies not in the mere possession of money; it lies in the joy of achievement, in the thrill of creative effort. The joy and moral stimulation of work no longer must be forgotten in the mad chase of evanescent profits. These dark days will be worth all they cost us if they teach us that our true destiny is not to be ministered unto but to minister to ourselves and to our fellow men.

Recognition of the falsity of material weath as the standard of success goes hand in hand with the abandonment of the false belief that public office and high political position are to be valued only by the standards of pride of place and personal profit; and there must be an end to a conduct in banking and in business which too often has given to a sacred trust the likeness of callous and selfish wrongdoing. Small wonder that confidence languishes, for it thrives only on honesty, on honor, on the sacredness of obligations, on faithful protection, on unselfish performance; without them it cannot live.

Restoration calls, however, not for changes in ethics alone. This Nation asks for action, and action now.

Our greatest primary task is to put people to work. This is no unsolvable problem if we face it wisely and courageously. It can be accomplished in part by direct recruiting by the Government itself, treating the task as we would treat the emergency of a war, but at the same time, through this employment, accomplishing greatly needed projects to stimulate and reorganize the use of our natural resources.

Hand in hand with this we must frankly recognize the overbalance of population in our industrial centers and, by engaging on a national scale in a redistribution, endeavor to provide a better use of the land for those best fitted for the land. The task can be helped by definite efforts to raise the values of agricultural products and with this the power to purchase the output of our cities. It can be helped by preventing realistically the tragedy of the growing loss through foreclosure of our small homes and our farms. It can be helped by insistence that the Federal, State, and local governments act forthwith on the demand that their cost be drastically reduced. It can be helped by the unifying of relief activities which today are often scattered, uneconomical, and unequal. It can be helped by national planning for and supervision of all forms of transportation and of communications and other utilities which have a definitely public character. There are many ways in which it can be helped, but it can never be helped merely by talking about it. We must act and act quickly.

Finally, in our progress toward a resumption of work we require two safeguards against a return of the evils of the old order; there must be a strict supervision of all banking and credits and investments, so that there will be an end to speculation with other people's money; and there must be provision for an adequate but sound currency.

These are the lines of attack. I shall presently urge upon a new Congress, in special session, detailed measures for their fulfillment, and I shall seek the immediate assistance of the several States.

Through this program of action we address ourselves to putting our national house in order and making income balance outgo. Our international trade relations, though vastly important, are in point of time and necessity secondary to the establishment of a sound national economy. I favor as a practical policy the putting of first things first. I shall spare no effort to restore world trade by international economic readjustment, but the emergency at home cannot wait on that accomplishment.

The basic thought that guides these specific means of national recovery is not narrowly nationalistic. It is the insistence, as a first consideration, upon the interdependence of the various elements in and part of the United States—a recognition of the old and permanently important manifestation of the American spirit of the pioneer. It is the way to recovery. It is the immediate way. It is the strongest assurance that the recovery will endure.

In the field of world policy I would dedicate this Nation to the policy of the good neighbor—the neighbor who resolutely respects himself and, because he does so, respects the rights of others—the neighbor who respects his obligations and respects the sanctity of his agreements in and with a world of neighbors.

If I read the temper of our people correctly, we now realize as we have never realized before our interdependence on each other; that we cannot merely take but we must give as well; that if we are to go forward, we must move as a trained and loyal army willing to sacrifice for the good of a common discipline, because without such discipline no progress is made, no leadership becomes effective. We are, I know, ready and willing to submit our lives and property to such discipline, because it makes possible a leadership which aims at a larger good. This I propose to offer, pledging that the larger purposes will bind upon us all as a sacred obligation with a unity of duty hitherto evoked only in time of armed strife.

With this pledge taken, I assume unhesitatingly the leadership of this great army of our people dedicated to a disciplined attack upon our common problems.

Action in this image and to this end is feasible under the form of government which we have inherited from our ancestors. Our Constitution is so simple and practical that it is possible always to meet extraordinary needs by changes in emphasis and arrangement without loss of essential form. That is why our constitutional system has proved itself the most superbly enduring political mechanism the modern world has produced. It has met every stress of vast expansion of territory, of foreign wars, of bitter internal strife, of world relations.

It is to be hoped that the normal balance of Executive and legislative authority may be wholly adequate to meet the unprecedented task before us. But it may be that an unprecedented demand and need for undelayed action may call for temporary departure from that normal balance of public procedure.

I am prepared under my constitutional duty to recommend the measures that a stricken Nation in the midst of a stricken world may require. These measures, or such other measures as the Congress may build out of its experience and wisdom, I shall seek, within my constitutional authority, to bring to speedy adoption.

But in the event that the Congress shall fail to take one of these two courses, and in the event that the national emergency is still critical, I shall not evade the clear course of duty that will then confront me. I shall ask the Congress for the one remaining instrument to meet the crisis—broad Executive power to wage a war against the emergency, as great as the power that would be given to me if we were in fact invaded by a foreign foe.

For the trust reposed in me I will return the courage and the devotion that befit the time. I can do no less.

We face the arduous days that lie before us in the warm courage of national unity; with the clear consciousness of seeking old and precious moral values; with the clean satisfaction that comes from the stern performance of duty by old and young alike. We aim at the assurance of a rounded and permanent national life.

We do not distrust the future of essential democracy. The people of the United States have not failed. In their need they have registered a mandate that they want direct, vigorous action. They have asked for discipline and direction under leadership. They have made me the present instrument of their wishes. In the spirit of the gift I take it.

In this dedication of a Nation we humbly ask the blessing of God. May He protect each and every one of us. May He guide me in the days to come.

FIRST FIRESIDE CHAT
March 12, 1933

I want to talk for a few minutes with the people of the United States about banking—with the comparatively few who understand the mechanics of banking but more particularly with the overwhelming majority who use banks for the making of deposits and the drawing of checks. I want to tell you what has been done in the last few days, why it was done, and what the next steps are going to be. I recognize that the many proclamations from State capitols and from Washington, the legislation, the Treasury regulations, etc., couched for the most part in banking and legal terms, should be explained for the benefit of the average citizen. I owe this in particular because of the fortitude and good temper with which everybody has accepted the inconvenience and hardships of the banking holiday. I know that when you understand what we in Washington have been about I shall continue to have your cooperation as fully as I have had your sympathy and help during the past week.

First of all, let me state the simple fact that when you deposit money in a bank the bank does not put the money into a safe deposit vault. It invests your money in many different forms of credit —bonds, commercial paper, mortgages and many other kinds of loans. In other words, the bank puts your money to work to keep the wheels of industry and of agriculture turning around. A comparatively small part of the money you put into the bank is kept in currency—an amount which in normal times is wholly sufficient to cover the cash needs of the average citizen. In other words, the total amount of all the currency in the country is only a small fraction of the total deposits in all of the banks.

What, then, happened during the last few days of February and the first few days of March? Because of undermined confidence on the part of the public, there was a general rush by a large portion of our population to turn bank deposits into currency or gold—a rush so great that the soundest banks could not get enough currency to meet the demand. The reason for this was that on the spur of the moment it was, of course, impossible to sell perfectly sound assets of a bank and convert them into cash except at panic prices far below their real value.

By the afternoon of March 3d scarcely a bank in the country was open to do business. Proclamations temporarily closing them in whole or in part had been issued by the Governors in almost all the States.

It was then that I issued the proclamation providing for the nation-wide bank holiday, and this was the first step in the Government's reconstruction of our financial and economic fabric.

The second step was the legislation promptly and patriotically passed by the Congress confirming my proclamation and broadening my powers so that it became possible in view of the requirement of time to extend the holiday and lift the ban of that holiday gradually. This law also gave authority to develop a program of rehabilitation of our banking facilities. I want to tell our citizens in every part of the Nation that the national Congress—Republicans and Democrats alike—showed by this action a devotion to public welfare and a realization of the emergency and the necessity for speed that it is difficult to match in our history.

The third stage has been the series of regulations permitting the banks to continue their functions to take care of the distribution of food and household necessities and the payment of payrolls.

This bank holiday, while resulting in many cases in great inconvenience, is affording us the opportunity to supply the currency necessary to meet the situation. No sound bank is a dollar worse off than it was when it closed its doors last Monday. Neither is any bank which may turn out not to be in a position for immediate opening. The new law allows the twelve Federal Reserve Banks to issue additional currency on good assets and thus the banks which reopen will be able to meet every legitimate call. The new currency is being sent out by the Bureau of Engraving and Printing in large volume to every part of the country. It is sound currency because it is backed by actual, good assets.

A question you will ask is this: why are all the banks not to be reopened at the same time? The answer is simple. Your Government does not intend that the history of the past few years shall be repeated. We do not want and will not have another epidemic of bank failures.

As a result, we start tomorrow, Monday, with the opening of banks in the twelve Federal Reserve Bank cities—those banks which on first examination by the Treasury have already been found to be all right. This will be followed on Tuesday by the resumption of all their functions by banks already found to be sound in cities where there are recognized clearing houses. That means about 250 cities of the United States.

On Wednesday and succeeding days banks in smaller places all through the country will resume business, subject, of course, to the Government's physical ability to complete its survey. It is necessary that the reopening of banks be extended over a period in order to permit the banks to make applications for necessary loans, to obtain currency needed to meet their requirements and to enable the Government to make common sense checkups.

Let me make it clear to you that if your bank does not open the first day you are by no means justified in believing that it will not open. A bank that opens on one of the subsequent days is in exactly the same status as the bank that opens tomorrow.

I know that many people are worrying about State banks not members of the Federal Reserve System. These banks can and will receive assistance from member banks and from the Reconstruction Finance Corporation. These State banks are following the same course as the National banks except that they get their licenses to resume business from the State authorities, and these authorities have been asked by the Secretary of the Treasury to permit their good banks to open up on the same schedule as the national banks. I am confident that the State Banking Departments will be as careful as the national Government in the policy relating to the opening of banks and will follow the same broad policy.

It is possible that when the banks resume a very few people who have not recovered from their fear may again begin withdrawals. Let me make it clear that the banks will take care of all needs—and it is my belief that hoarding during the past week has become an exceedingly unfashionable pastime. It needs no prophet to tell you that when the people find that they can get their money—that they can get it when they want it for all legitimate purposes—the phantom of fear will soon be laid. People will again be glad to have their money where it will be safely taken care of and where they can use it conveniently at any time. I can assure you that it is safer to keep your money in a reopened bank than under the mattress.

The success of our whole great national program depends, of course, upon the cooperation of the public—on its intelligent support and use of a reliable system.

Remember that the essential accomplishment of the new legislation is that it makes it possible for banks more readily to convert their assets into cash than was the case before. More liberal provision has been made for banks to borrow on these assets at the Reserve Banks and more liberal provision has also been made for issuing currency on the security of these good assets. This currency is not fiat currency. It is issued only on adequate security, and every good bank has an abundance of such security.

One more point before I close. There will be, of course, some banks unable to reopen without being reorganized. The new law allows the Government to assist in making their reorganizations quickly and effectively and even allows the Government to subscribe to at least a part of new capital which may be required.

I hope you can see from this elemental recital of what your Government is doing that there is nothing complex, or radical, in the process.

We had a bad banking situation. Some of our bankers had shown themselves either incompetent or dishonest in their handling of the people's funds. They had used the money entrusted to them in speculations and unwise loans. This was, of course, not true in the vast majority of our banks, but it was true in enough of them to shock the people for a time into a sense of insecurity and to put them into a frame of mind where they did not differentiate, but seemed to assume that the acts of a comparative few had tainted them all. It was the Government's job to straighten out this situation and do it as quickly as possible. And the job is being performed.

I do not promise you that every bank will be reopened or that individual losses will not be suffered, but there will be no losses that possibly could be avoided; and there would have been more and greater losses had we continued to drift. I can even promise you salvation for some at least of the sorely pressed banks. We shall be engaged not merely in reopening sound banks but in the creation of sound banks through reorganization.

It has been wonderful to me to catch the note of confidence from all over the country. I can never be sufficiently grateful to the people for the loyal support they have given me in their acceptance of the judgment that has dictated our course, even though all our processes may not have seemed clear to them.

After all, there is an element in the readjustment of our financial system more important than currency, more important than gold, and that is the confidence of the people. Confidence and courage are the essentials of success in carrying out our plan. You people must have faith, you must not be stampeded by rumors or guesses. Let us unite in banishing fear. We have provided the machinery to restore our financial system; it is up to you to support and make it work.

It is your problem no less than it is mine. Together we cannot fail.

SECOND FIRESIDE CHAT
May 7, 1933

On a Sunday night a week after my inauguration I used the radio to tell you about the banking crisis and the measures we were taking to meet it. I think that in that way I made clear to the country various facts that might otherwise have been misunderstood and in general provided a means of understanding which did much to restore confidence.

Tonight, eight weeks later, I come for the second time to give you my report; in the same spirit and by the same means to tell you about what we have been doing and what we are planning to do.

Two months ago we were facing serious problems. The country was dying by inches. It was dying because trade and commerce had declined to dangerously low levels; prices for basic commodities were such as to destroy the value of the assets of national institutions such as banks, savings banks, insurance companies, and others. These institutions, because of their great needs, were foreclosing mortgages, calling loans, refusing credit. Thus there was actually in process of destruction the property of millions of people who had borrowed money on that property in terms of dollars which had had an entirely different value from the level of March, 1933. That situation in that crisis did not call for any complicated consideration of economic panaceas or fancy plans. We were faced by a condition and not a theory.

There were just two alternatives: The first was to allow the foreclosures to continue, credit to be withheld and money to go into hiding, thus forcing liquidation and bankruptcy of banks, railroads and insurance companies and a recapitalizing of all business and all property on a lower level. This alternative meant a continuation of what is loosely called "deflation," the net result of which would have been extraordinary hardships on all property owners and, incidentally, extraordinary hardships on all persons working for wages through an increase in unemployment and a further reduction of the wage scale.

It is easy to see that the result of this course would have not only economic effects of a very serious nature, but social results that might bring incalculable harm. Even before I was inaugurated I came to the conclusion that such a policy was too much to ask the American people to bear. It involved not only a further loss of homes, farms, savings and wages, but also a loss of spiritual values —the loss of that sense of security for the present and the future so necessary to the peace and contentment of the individual and of his family. When you destroy these things you will find it difficult to establish confidence of any sort in the future. It was clear that mere appeals from Washington for confidence and the mere lending of more money to shaky institutions could not stop this downward course. A prompt program applied as quickly as possible seemed to me not only justified but imperative to our national security. The Congress, and when I say Congress I mean the members of both political parties, fully understood this and gave me generous and intelligent support. The members of Congress realized that the methods of normal times had to be replaced in the emergency by measures which were suited to the serious and pressing requirements of the moment. There was no actual surrender of power. Congress still retained its constitutional authority, and no one has the slightest desire to change the balance of these powers. The function of Congress is to decide what has to be done and to select the appropriate agency to carry out its will. To this policy it has strictly adhered. The only thing that has been happening has been to designate the President as the agency to carry out certain of the purposes of the Congress. This was constitutional and in keeping with the past American tradition.

The legislation which has been passed or is in the process of enactment can properly be considered as part of a well-grounded plan.

First, we are giving opportunity of employment to one-quarter of a million of the unemployed, especially the young men who have dependents, to go into the forestry and flood-prevention work. This is a big task because it means feeding, clothing and caring for nearly twice as many men as we have in the regular army itself. In creating this civilian conservation corps we are killing two birds with one stone. We are clearly enhancing the value of our natural resources, and we are relieving an appreciable amount of actual distress. This great group of men has entered upon its work on a purely voluntary basis; no military training is involved and we are conserving not only our natural resources, but our human resources. One of the great values to this work is the fact that it is direct and requires the intervention of very little machinery.

Second, I have requested the Congress and have secured action upon a proposal to put the great properties owned by our Government at Muscle Shoals to work after long years of wasteful inaction, and with this a broad plan for the improvement of a vast area in the Tennessee Valley. It will add to the comfort and happiness of hundreds of thousands of people and the incident benefits will reach the entire Nation.

Next, the Congress is about to pass legislation that will greatly ease the mortgage distress among the farmers and the home owners of the Nation, by providing for the easing of the burden of debt now bearing so heavily upon millions of our people.

Our next step in seeking immediate relief is a grant of half a billion dollars to help the States, counties and municipalities in their duty to care for those who need direct and immediate relief.

The Congress also passed legislation authorizing the sale of beer in such States as desired it. This has already resulted in considerable reemployment and incidentally has provided much-needed tax revenue.

We are planning to ask the Congress for legislation to enable the Government to undertake public works, thus stimulating directly and indirectly the employment of many others in well-considered projects.

Further legislation has been taken up which goes much more fundamentally into our economic problems. The Farm Relief Bill seeks by the use of several methods, alone or together, to bring about an increased return to farmers for their major farm products, seeking at the same time to prevent in the days to come disastrous overproduction which so often in the past has kept farm commodity prices far below a reasonable return. This measure provides wide powers for emergencies. The extent of its use will depend entirely upon what the future has in store.

Well-considered and conservative measures will likewise be proposed which will attempt to give to the industrial workers of the country a more fair wage return, prevent cut-throat competition and unduly long hours for labor, and at the same time encourage each industry to prevent overproduction.

Our Railroad Bill falls into the same class because it seeks to provide and make certain definite planning by the railroads themselves, with the assistance of the Government, to eliminate the duplication and waste that is now resulting in railroad receiverships and continuing operating deficits.

I am certain that the people of this country understand and approve the broad purposes behind these new governmental policies relating to agriculture and industry and transportation. We found ourselves faced with more agricultural products than we could possibly consume ourselves, and with surpluses which other Nations did not have the cash to buy from us except at prices ruinously low. We found our factories able to turn out more goods than we could possibly consume, and at the same time we were faced with a falling export demand. We found ourselves with more facilities to transport goods and crops than there were goods and crops to be transported. All of this has been caused in large part by a complete lack of planning and a complete failure to understand the danger signals that have been flying ever since the close of the World War. The people of this country have been erroneously encouraged to believe that they could keep on increasing the output of farm and factory indefinitely and that some magician would find ways and means for that increased output to be consumed with reasonable profit to the producer.

Today we have reason to believe that things are a little better than they were two months ago. Industry has picked up, railroads are carrying more freight, farm prices are better, but I am not going to indulge in issuing proclamations of over-enthusiastic assurance. We cannot ballyhoo ourselves back to prosperity. I am going to be honest at all times with the people of the country. I do not want the people of this country to take the foolish course of letting this improvement come back on another speculative wave. I do not want the people to believe that because of unjustified optimism we can resume the ruinous practice of increasing our crop output and our factory output in the hope that a kind Providence will find buyers at high prices. Such a course may bring us immediate and false prosperity but it will be the kind of prosperity that will lead us into another tailspin.

It is wholly wrong to call the measures that we have taken Governmental control of farming, industry, and transportation. It is rather a partnership between Government and farming and industry and transportation, not partnership in profits, for the profits still go to citizens, but rather a partnership in planning, and a partnership to see that the plans are carried out.

Let me illustrate with an example. Take the cotton-goods industry. It is probably true that 90 percent of the cotton manufacturers would agree to eliminate starvation wages, would agree to stop long hours of employment, would agree to stop child labor, would agree to prevent an overproduction that would result in unsalable surpluses. But, what good is such an agreement if the other 10 percent of cotton manufacturers pay starvation wages, require long hours, employ children in their mills and turn out burdensome surpluses? The unfair 10 percent could produce goods so cheaply that the fair 90 percent would be compelled to meet the unfair conditions. Here is where the Government comes in. Government ought to have the right and will have the right, after surveying and planning for an industry, to prevent, with the assistance of the overwhelming majority of that industry, unfair practices and to enforce this agreement by the authority of Government. The so-called antitrust laws were intended to prevent the creation of monopolies and to forbid unreasonable profits to those monopolies. That purpose of the anti-trust laws must be continued, but these laws were never intended to encourage the kind of unfair competition that results in long hours, starvation wages and overproduction.

The same principle applies to farm products and to transportation and every other field of organized private industry.

We are working toward a definite goal, which is to prevent the return of conditions which came very close to destroying what we call modern civilization. The actual accomplishment of our purpose cannot be attained in a day. Our policies are wholly within purposes for which our American Constitutional Government was established 150 years ago.

I know that the people of this country will understand this and will also understand the spirit in which we are undertaking this policy. I do not deny that we may make mistakes of procedure as we carry out the policy. I have no expectation of making a hit every time I come to bat. What I seek is the highest possible batting average, not only for myself but for the team. Theodore Roosevelt once said to me: "If I can be right 75 percent of the time I shall come up to the fullest measure of my hopes."

Much has been said of late about Federal finances and inflation, the gold standard, etc. Let me make the facts very simple and my policy very clear. In the first place, Government credit and Government currency are really one and the same thing. Behind Government bonds there is only a promise to pay. Behind Government currency we have, in addition to the promise to pay, a reserve of gold and a small reserve of silver. In this connection it is worth while remembering that in the past the Government has agreed to redeem nearly thirty billions of its debts and its currency in gold, and private corporations in this country have agreed to redeem another sixty or seventy billions of securities and mortgages in gold. The Government and private corporations were making these agreements when they knew full well that all of the gold in the United States amounted to only between three and four billions and that all of the gold in all of the world amounted to only about eleven billions.

If the holders of these promises to pay started in to demand gold the first comers would get gold for a few days and they would amount to about one-twenty-fifth of the holders of the securities and the currency. The other twenty-four people out of twenty-five, who did not happen to be at the top of the line, would be told politely that there was no more gold left. We have decided to treat all twenty-five in the same way in the interest of justice and the exercise of the constitutional powers of this Government. We have placed everyone on the same basis in order that the general good may be preserved.

Nevertheless, gold, and to a partial extent silver, are perfectly good bases for currency, and that is why I decided not to let any of the gold now in the country go out of it.

A series of conditions arose three weeks ago which very readily might have meant, first, a drain on our gold by foreign countries, and second, as a result of that, a flight of American capital, in the form of gold, out of our country. It is not exaggerating the possibility to tell you that such an occurrence might well have taken from us the major part of our gold reserve and resulted in such a further weakening of our Government and private credit as to bring on actual panic conditions and the complete stoppage of the wheels of industry.

The Administration has the definite objective of raising commodity prices to such an extent that those who have borrowed money will, on the average, be able to repay that money in the same kind of dollar which they borrowed. We do not seek to let them get such a cheap dollar that they will be able to pay back a great deal less than they borrowed. In other words, we seek to correct a wrong and not to create another wrong in the opposite direction. That is why powers are being given to the Administration to provide, if necessary, for an enlargement of credit, in order to correct the existing wrong. These powers will be used when, as, and if it may be necessary to accomplish the purpose.

Hand in hand with the domestic situation which, of course, is our first concern is the world situation, and I want to emphasize to you that the domestic situation is inevitably and deeply tied in with the conditions in all of the other Nations of the world. In other words, we can get, in all probability, a fair measure of prosperity to return in the United States, but it will not be permanent unless we get a return to prosperity all over the world.

In the conferences which we have held and are holding with the leaders of other Nations, we are seeking four great objectives: first, a general reduction of armaments and through this the removal of the fear of invasion and armed attack, and, at the same time, a reduction in armament costs, in order to help in the balancing of Government budgets and the reduction of taxation; second, a cutting down of the trade barriers, in order to restart the flow of exchange of crops and goods between Nations; third, the setting up of a stabilization of currencies, in order that trade can make contracts ahead; fourth, the reestablishment of friendly relations and greater confidence between all Nations.

Our foreign visitors these past three weeks have responded to these purposes in a very helpful way. All of the Nations have suffered alike in this great depression. They have all reached the conclusion that each can best be helped by the common action of all. It is in this spirit that our visitors have met with us and discussed our common problems. The international conference that lies before us must succeed. The future of the world demands it and we have each of us pledged ourselves to the best joint efforts to this end.

To you, the people of this country, all of us, the members of the Congress and the members of this Administration, owe a profound debt of gratitude. Throughout the depression you have been patient. You have granted us wide powers; you have encouraged us with a widespread approval of our purposes. Every ounce of strength and every resource at our command we have devoted to the end of justifying your confidence. We are encouraged to believe that a wise and sensible beginning has been made. In the present spirit of mutual confidence and mutual encouragement we go forward.

THIRD FIRESIDE CHAT
July 24, 1933

After the adjournment of the historical special session of the Congress five weeks ago I purposely refrained from addressing you for two very good reasons.

First, I think that we all wanted the opportunity of a little quiet thought to examine and assimilate in a mental picture the crowding events of the hundred days which had been devoted to the starting of the wheels of the New Deal.

Secondly, I wanted a few weeks in which to set up the new administrative organization and to see the first fruits of our careful planning.

I think it will interest you if I set forth the fundamentals of this planning for national recovery; and this I am very certain will make it abundantly clear to you that all of the proposals and all of the legislation since the fourth day of March have not been just a collection of haphazard schemes, but rather the orderly component parts of a connected and logical whole.

Long before Inauguration Day I became convinced that individual effort and local effort and even disjointed Federal effort had failed and of necessity would fail and, therefore, that a rounded leadership by the Federal Government had become a necessity both of theory and of fact. Such leadership, however, had its beginning in preserving and strengthening the credit of the United States Government, because without that no leadership was a possibility. For years the Government had not lived within its income. The immediate task was to bring our regular expenses within our revenues. That has been done.

It may seem inconsistent for a government to cut down its regular expenses and at the same time to borrow and to spend billions for an emergency. But it is not inconsistent because a large portion of the emergency money has been paid out in the form of sound loans which will be repaid to the Treasury over a period of years; and to cover the rest of the emergency money we have imposed taxes to pay the interest and the installments on that part of the debt.

So you will see that we have kept our credit good. We have built a granite foundation in a period of confusion. That foundation of the Federal credit stands there broad and sure. It is the base of the whole recovery plan.

Then came the part of the problem that concerned the credit of the individual citizens themselves. You and I know of the banking crisis and of the great danger to the savings of our people. On March sixth every national bank was closed. One month later 90 per cent of the deposits in the national banks had been made available to the depositors. Today only about 5 per cent of the deposits in national banks are still tied up. The condition relating to State banks, while not quite so good on a percentage basis, is showing a steady reduction in the total of frozen deposits—a result much better than we had expected three months ago.

The problem of the credit of the individual was made more difficult because of another fact. The dollar was a different dollar from the one with which the average debt had been incurred. For this reason large numbers of people were actually losing possession of and title to their farms and homes. All of you know the financial steps which have been taken to correct this inequality. In addition the Home Loan Act, the Farm Loan Act and the Bankruptcy Act were passed.

It was a vital necessity to restore purchasing power by reducing the debt and interest charges upon our people, but while we were helping people to save their credit it was at the same time absolutely essential to do something about the physical needs of hundreds of thousands who were in dire straits at that very moment. Municipal and State aid were being stretched to the limit. We appropriated half a billion dollars to supplement their efforts and in addition, as you know, we have put 300,000 young men into practical and useful work in our forests and to prevent flood and soil erosion. The wages they earn are going in greater part to the support of the nearly one million people who constitute their families.

In this same classification we can properly place the great public works program running to a total of over three billion dollars—to be used for highways and ships and flood prevention and inland navigation and thousands of self-sustaining State and municipal improvements. Two points should be made clear in the allotting and administration of these projects: first, we are using the utmost care to choose labor-creating, quick-acting, useful projects, avoiding the smell of the pork barrel; and second, we are hoping that at least half of the money will come back to the Government from projects which will pay for themselves over a period of years.

Thus far I have spoken primarily of the foundation stones—the measures that were necessary to reestablish credit and to head people in the opposite direction by preventing distress and providing as much work as possible through governmental agencies. Now I come to the links which will build us a more lasting prosperity. I have said that we cannot attain that in a Nation half boom and half broke. If all of our people have work and fair wages and fair profits, they can buy the products of their neighbors, and business is good. But if you take away the wages and the profits of half of them, business is only half as good. It does not help much if the fortunate half is very prosperous; the best way is for everybody to be reasonably prosperous.

For many years the two great barriers to a normal prosperity have been low farm prices and the creeping paralysis of unemployment. These factors have cut the purchasing power of the country in half. I promised action. Congress did its part when it passed the Farm and the Industrial Recovery Acts. Today we are putting these two Acts to work and they will work if people understand their plain objectives.

First, the Farm Act: It is based on the fact that the purchasing power of nearly half of our population depends on adequate prices for farm products. We have been producing more of some crops than we consume or can sell in a depressed world market. The cure is not to produce so much. Without our help the farmers cannot get together and cut production, and the Farm Bill gives them a method of bringing their production down to a reasonable level and of obtaining reasonable prices for their crops. I have clearly stated that this method is in a sense experimental, but so far as we have gone we have reason to believe that it will produce good results.

It is obvious that if we can greatly increase the purchasing power of the tens of millions of our people who make a living from farming and the distribution of farm crops, we shall greatly increase the consumption of those goods which are turned out by industry.

That brings me to the final step—bringing back industry along sound lines.

Last Autumn, on several occasions, I expressed my faith that we can make possible by democratic self-discipline in industry general increases in wages and shortening of hours sufficient to enable industry to pay its own workers enough to let those workers buy and use the things that their labor produces. This can be done only if we permit and encourage cooperative action in industry, because it is obvious that without united action a few selfish men in each competitive group will pay starvation wages and insist on long hours of work. Others in that group must either follow suit or close up shop. We have seen the result of action of that kind in the continuing descent into the economic hell of the past four years.

There is a clear way to reverse that process: If all employers in each competitive group agree to pay their workers the same wages—reasonable wages—and require the same hours—reasonable hours—then higher wages and shorter hours will hurt no employer. Moreover, such action is better for the employer than unemployment and low wages, because it makes more buyers for his product. That is the simple idea which is the very heart of the Industrial Recovery Act.

On the basis of this simple principle of everybody doing things together, we are starting out on this nationwide attack on unemployment. It will succeed if our people understand it—in the big industries, in the little shops, in the great cities and in the small villages. There is nothing complicated about it and there is nothing particularly new in the principle. It goes back to the basic idea of society and of the Nation itself that people acting in a group can accomplish things which no individual acting alone could even hope to bring about.

Here is an example. In the Cotton Textile Code and in other agreements already signed, child labor has been abolished. That makes me personally happier than any other one thing with which I have been connected since I came to Washington. In the textile industry—an industry which came to me spontaneously and with a splendid cooperation as soon as the Recovery Act was signed—child labor was an old evil. But no employer acting alone was able to wipe it out. If one employer tried it, or if one State tried it, the costs of operation rose so high that it was impossible to compete with the employers of States which had failed to act. The moment the Recovery Act was passed, this monstrous thing which neither opinion nor law could reach through years of effort went out in a flash. As a British editorial put it, we did more under a Code in one day than they in England had been able to do under the common law in eighty-five years of effort. I use this incident, my friends, not to boast of what has already been done but to point the way to you for even greater cooperative efforts this summer and autumn.

We are not going through another winter like the last. I doubt if ever any people so bravely and cheerfully endured a season half so bitter. We cannot ask America to continue to face such needless hardships. It is time for courageous action, and the Recovery Bill gives us the means to conquer unemployment with exactly the same weapon that we have used to strike down child labor.

The proposition is simply this:

If all employers will act together to shorten hours and raise wages we can put people back to work. No employer will suffer, because the relative level of competitive cost will advance by the same amount for all. But if any considerable group should lag or shirk, this great opportunity will pass us by and we shall go into another desperate winter. This must not happen.

We have sent out to all employers an agreement which is the result of weeks of consultation. This agreement checks against the voluntary codes of nearly all the large industries which have already been submitted. This blanket agreement carries the unanimous approval of the three boards which I have appointed to advise in this, boards representing the great leaders in labor, in industry, and in social service. The agreement has already brought a flood of approval from every State, and from so wide a cross-section of the common calling of industry that I know it is fair for all. It is a plan —deliberate, reasonable and just—intended to put into effect at once the most important of the broad principles which are being established, industry by industry, through codes. Naturally, it takes a good deal of organizing and a great many hearings and many months, to get these codes perfected and signed, and we cannot wait for all of them to go through. The blanket agreements, however, which I am sending to every employer will start the wheels turning now, and not six months from now.

There are, of course, men, a few men, who might thwart this great common purpose by seeking selfish advantage. There are adequate penalties in the law, but I am now asking the cooperation that comes from opinion and from conscience. These are the only instruments we shall use in this great summer offensive against unemployment. But we shall use them to the limit to protect the willing from the laggard and to make the plan succeed.

In war, in the gloom of night attack, soldiers wear a bright badge on their shoulders to be sure that comrades do not fire on comrades. On that principle, those who cooperate in this program must know each other at a glance. That is why we have provided a badge of honor for this purpose, a simple design with a legend, "We do our part," and I ask that all those who join with me shall display that badge prominently. It is essential to our purpose.

Already all the great, basic industries have come forward willingly with proposed codes, and in these codes they accept the principles leading to mass reemployment. But, important as is this heartening demonstration, the richest field for results is among the small employers, those whose contribution will be to give new work for from one to ten people. These smaller employers are indeed a vital part of the backbone of the country, and the success of our plan lies largely in their hands.

Already the telegrams and letters are pouring into the White House—messages from employers who ask that their names be placed on this special Roll of Honor. They represent great corporations and companies, and partnerships and individuals. I ask that even before the dates set in the agreements which we have sent

out, the employers of the country who have not already done so—
the big fellows and the little fellows—shall at once write or telegraph
to me personally at the White House, expressing their intentions of
going through with the plan. And it is my purpose to keep posted
in the post office of every town, a Roll of Honor of all those who
join with me.

I want to take this occasion to say to the twenty-four Governors
who are now in conference in San Francisco, that nothing thus far
has helped in strengthening this great movement more than their
resolutions adopted at the very outset of their meeting, giving this
plan their instant and unanimous approval, and pledging to support
it in their States.

To the men and women whose lives have been darkened by
the fact or the fear of unemployment, I am justified in saying a word
of encouragement because the codes and the agreements already
approved, or about to be passed upon, prove that the plan does raise
wages, and that it does put people back to work. You can look
on every employer who adopts the plan as one who is doing his part,
and those employers deserve well of everyone who works for a
living. It will be clear to you, as it is to me, that while the shirking
employer may undersell his competitor, the saving he thus makes is
made at the expense of his country's welfare.

While we are making this great common effort there should
be no discord and dispute. This is no time to cavil or to question
the standard set by this universal agreement. It is time for patience
and understanding and cooperation. The workers of this country
have rights under this law which cannot be taken from them, and
nobody will be permitted to whittle them away but, on the other
hand, no aggression is now necessary to attain those rights. The
whole country will be united to get them for you. The principle
that applies to the employers applies to the workers as well, and
I ask you workers to cooperate in the same spirit.

When Andrew Jackson, "Old Hickory," died, someone asked,
"Will he go to Heaven?" and the answer was, "He will if he wants
to." If I am asked whether the American people will pull themselves out of this depression, I answer, "They will if they want to."
The essence of the plan is a universal limitation of hours of work
per week for any individual by common consent, and a universal
payment of wages above a minimum, also by common consent. I
cannot guarantee the success of this nation-wide plan, but the people
of this country can guarantee its success. I have no faith in "cure-
alls" but I believe that we can greatly influence economic forces.
I have no sympathy with the professional economists who insist that
things must run their course and that human agencies can have no
influence on economic ills. One reason is that I happen to know that
professional economists have changed their definition of economic

laws every five or ten years for a very long time, but I do have faith, and retain faith, in the strength of the common purpose, and in the strength of unified action taken by the American people.

That is why I am describing to you the simple purposes and the solid foundations upon which our program of recovery is built. That is why I am asking the employers of the Nation to sign this common covenant with me—to sign it in the name of patriotism and humanity. That is why I am asking the workers to go along with us in a spirit of understanding and of helpfulness.

ADDRESS TO THE FEDERAL COUNCIL OF CHURCHES

"*The Right to a More Abundant Life*"

December 6, 1933

I am honored by the privilege of speaking to the delegated representatives of twenty-five Christian denominations assembled here on the twenty-fifth anniversary of the Federal Council of Churches of Christ in America. In this quarter of a century you have surrendered no individual creed, but at the same time you have been creating a much-needed union that seeks to better the social and moral conditions of all the people of America.

During a quarter of a century more greatly controlled by the spirit of conquest and greed than any similar period since the American and French Revolutions you have survived and grown. You have come through to the threshold of a new era in which your churches and the other churches—Gentile and Jewish—recognize and stand ready to lead in a new war of peace—the war for social justice.

Christianity was born in and of an era notable for the great gulf that separated the privileged from the underprivileged of the world of two thousand years ago—an era of lines of demarcation between conquerors and conquered; between caste and caste; beween warring philosophies based on the theories of logicians rather than on practical humanities. The early churches were united in a social ideal.

Although through all the centuries we know of many periods when civilization has slipped a step backward, yet I am confident that over the sum of the centuries we have gained many steps for every one we have lost.

Now, once more, we are embarking on another voyage into the realm of human contacts. That human agency which we call government is seeking through social and economic means the same goal which the churches are seeking through social and spiritual means.

If I were asked to state the great objective which Church and State are both demanding for the sake of every man and woman and child in this country, I would say that that great objective is "a more abundant life."

The early Christians challenged the pagan ethics of Greece and of Rome; we are wholly ready to challenge the pagan ethics that are represented in many phases of our boasted modern civilization. We have called on enlightened business judgment, on understanding labor and on intelligent agriculture to provide a more equitable balance of the abundant life between all elements of the community.

We recognize the right of the individual to seek and to obtain his own fair wage, his own fair profit, in his own fair way—just so long as in the doing of it he does not push down or hold down his own neighbor. And at the same time, we are at one in calling for collective effort on broad lines of social planning—a collective effort which is wholly in accord with the social teachings of Christianity.

This new generation of ours stands ready to help us. They may not be as ready as were their fathers and mothers to accept the outward requirements or even many of the ancient observances of the several churches, yet I truly believe that these same churches can find in them a stronger support for the fundamentals of social betterment than many of the older generation are willing to concede.

This younger generation is not satisfied with the exposure of those in high places who seek to line their own nests with other people's money, to cheat their Government of its just dues or to break the spirit of the law while observing its legalistic letter. This new generation seeks action—action by collective government and by individual education, toward the ending of practices such as these.

This new generation, for example, is not content with preachings against that vile form of collective murder—lynch law—which has broken out in our midst anew. We know that it is murder, and a deliberate and definite disobedience of the Commandment, "Thou shalt not kill." We do not excuse those in high places or low who condone lynch law.

But a thinking America goes farther. It seeks a Government of its own that will be sufficiently strong to protect the prisoner and at the same time to crystallize a public opinion so clear that Government of all kinds will be compelled to practice a more certain justice. The judicial function of government is the protection of the individual and of the community through quick and certain justice. That function in many places has fallen into a sad state of disrepair. It must be a part of our program to reestablish it.

From the bottom of my heart I believe that this beloved country of ours is entering upon a time of great gain. That gain can well include a greater material prosperity if we can take care that it is a prosperity for a hundred and twenty million human beings and not a prosperity for the top of the pyramid alone. It can be a prosperity socially controlled for the common good. It can be a prosperity built on spiritual and social values rather than on special privilege and special power.

Toward that new definition of prosperity the churches and the Governments, while wholly separate in their functioning, can work hand in hand. Government can ask the church to stress in their teaching the ideals of social jutsice, while at the same time government guarantees to the churches—Gentile and Jewish—the right to worship God in their own way. The churches, while they remain wholly free from even the suggestion of interference in Government, can at the same time teach their millions of followers that they have the right to demand of the Government of their own choosing, the maintenance and furtherance of "a more abundant life." State and Church are rightly united in a common aim. With the help of God, we are on the road toward it.

FOURTH FIRESIDE CHAT
June 28, 1934

It has been several months since I have talked with you concerning the problems of Government. Since January, those of us in whom you have vested responsibility have been engaged in the fulfillment of plans and policies which had been widely discussed in previous months. It seemed to us our duty not only to make the right path clear, but also to tread that path.

As we review the achievements of this session of the Seventy-third Congress, it is made increasingly clear that its task was essentially that of completing and fortifying the work it had begun in March, 1933. That was no easy task, but the Congress was equal to it. It has been well said that while there were a few exceptions, this Congress displayed a greater freedom from mere partisanship than any other peace-time Congress since the Administration of President Washington himself. The session was distinguished by the extent and variety of legislation enacted and by the intelligence and good-will of debate upon these measures.

I mention only a few of the major enactments. It provided for the readjustment of the debt burden through the corporate and municipal bankruptcy acts and the Farm Relief Act. It lent a hand to industry by encouraging loans to solvent industries unable to secure adequate help from banking institutions. It strengthened the integrity of finance through the regulation of securities exchanges. It provided a rational method of increasing our volume of foreign trade through reciprocal trading agreements. It strengthened our naval forces to conform with the intentions and permission of existing treaty rights. It made further advances toward peace in industry through the Labor Adjustment Act. It supplemented our agricultural policy through measures widely demanded by farmers themselves and intended to avert price-destroying surpluses. It strengthened the hand of the Federal Government in its attempts to suppress gangster crime. It took definite steps toward a national housing program through an act which I signed today designed t encourage private capital in the rebuilding of the homes of the Nation. It created a permanent Federal body for the just regulation of all forms of communication, including the telephone, the telegraph and the radio. Finally, and I believe most important, it reorganized, simplified and made more fair and just our monetary system, setting up standards and policies adequate to meet the necessities of modern economic life, doing justice to both gold and silver as the metal bases behind the currency of the United States.

In the consistent development of our previous efforts toward the saving and safeguarding of our national life, I have continued to recognize three related steps. The first was relief, because the primary concern of any Government dominated by the humane ideals of democracy is the simple principle that in a land of vast resources no one should be permitted to starve. Relief was and continues to be our first consideration. It calls for large expenditures and will continue in modified form to do so for a long time to come. We may as well recognize that fact. It comes from the paralysis that arose as the after-effect of that unfortunate decade characterized by a mad chase for unearned riches, and an unwillingness of leaders in almost every walk of life to look beyond their own schemes and speculations. In our administration of relief we follow two principles: first, that direct giving shall, whenever possible, be supplemented by provision for useful and remunerative work and, second, that where families in their existing surroundings will in all human probability never find an opportunity for full self-maintenance, happiness and enjoyment, we shall try to give them a new chance in new surroundings.

The second step was recovery, and it is sufficient for me to ask each and every one of you to compare the situation in agriculture and in industry today with what it was fifteen months ago.

At the same time we have recognized the necessity of reform and reconstruction—reform because much of our trouble today and in the past few years has been due to a lack of understanding of the elementary principles of justice and fairness by those in whom leadership in business and finance was placed—reconstruction because new conditions in our economic life as well as old but neglected conditions had to be corrected.

Substantial gains well known to all of you have justified our course. I could cite statistics to you as unanswerable measures of our national progress—statistics to show the gain in the average weekly pay envelope of workers in the great majority of industries —statistics to show hundreds of thousands reemployed in private industries, and other hundreds of thousands given new employment through the expansion of direct and indirect Government assistance of many kinds, although, of course, there are those exceptions in professional pursuits whose economic improvement, of necessity, will be delayed. I also could cite statistics to show the great rise in the value of farm products—statistics to prove the demand for consumers' goods, ranging all the way from food and clothing to automobiles, and of late to prove the rise in the demand for durable goods—statistics to cover the great increase in bank deposits, and to show the scores of thousands of homes and of farms which have been saved from foreclosure.

But the simplest way for each of you to judge recovery lies in the plain facts of your own individual situation. Are you better off than you were last year? Are your debts less burdensome? Is your bank account more secure? Are your working conditions better? Is your faith in your own individual future more firmly grounded?

Also, let me put to you another simple question: Have you as an individual paid too high a price for these gains? Plausible self-seekers and theoretical die-hards will tell you of the loss of individual liberty. Answer this question also out of the facts of your own life. Have you lost any of your rights of liberty or constitutional freedom of action and choice? Turn to the Bill of Rights of the Constitution, which I have solemnly sworn to maintain and under which your freedom rests secure. Read each provision of that Bill of Rights and ask yourself whether you personally have suffered the impairment of a single jot of these great assurances. I have no question in my mind as to what your answer will be. The record is written in the experiences of your own personal lives.

In other words, it is not the overwhelming majority of the farmers or manufacturers or workers who deny the substantial gains of the past year. The most vociferous of the Doubting Thomases may be divided roughly into two groups: First, those who seek special political privilege and, second, those who seek special financial privilege. About a year ago I used as an illustration the 90 percent of the cotton manufacturers of the United States who wanted to do the right thing by their employees and by the public but were prevented from doing so by the 10 percent who undercut them by unfair practices and un-American standards. It is well for us to remember that humanity is a long way from being perfect and that a selfish minority in every walk of life—farming, business, finance and even Government service itself—will always continue to think of themselves first and their fellow beings second.

In the working out of a great national program which seeks the primary good of the greatest number, it is true that the toes of some people are being stepped on and are going to be stepped on. But these toes belong to the comparative few who seek to retain or to gain position or riches or both by some short cut which is harmful to the greater good.

In the execution of the powers conferred on it by Congress, the Administration needs and will tirelessly seek the best ability that the country affords. Public service offers better rewards in the opportunity for service than ever before in our history—not great salaries, but enough to live on. In the building of this service there are coming to us men and women with ability and courage from every part of the Union. The days of the seeking of mere party advantage through the misuse of public power are drawing to a close. We are increasingly demanding and getting devotion to the public service on the part of every member of the Administration, high and low.

The program of the last year is definitely in operation and that operation month by month is being made to fit into the web of old and new conditions. The process of evolution is well illustrated by the constant changes in detailed organization and method going on in the National Recovery Administration. With every passing month we are making strides in the orderly handling of the relationship between employees and employers. Conditions differ, of course, in almost every part of the country and in almost every industry. Temporary methods of adjustment are being replaced by more permanent machinery and, I am glad to say, by a growing recognition on the part of employers and employees of the desirability of maintaining fair relationships all around.

So also, while almost everybody has recognized the tremendous strides in the elimination of child labor, in the payment of not less than fair minimum wages and in the shortening of hours, we are still feeling our way in solving problems which relate to self-government in industry, especially where such self-government tends to eliminate the fair operation of competition.

In this same process of evolution we are keeping before us the objects of protecting, on the one hand, industry against chiselers within its own ranks, and, on the other hand, the consumer through the maintenance of reasonable competition for the prevention of the unfair sky-rocketing of retail prices.

But, in addition to this our immediate task, we must still look to the larger future. I have pointed out to the Congress that we are seeking to find the way once more to well-known, long-established but to some degree forgotten ideals and values. We seek the security of the men, women and children of the Nation.

That security involves added means of providing better homes for the people of the Nation. That is the first principle of our future program.

The second is to plan the use of land and water resources of this country to the end that the means of livelihood of our citizens may be more adequate to meet their daily needs.

And, finally, the third principle is to use the agencies of government to assist in the establishment of means to provide sound and adequate protection against the vicissitudes of modern life—in other words, social insurance.

Later in the year I hope to talk with you more fully about these plans.

A few timid people, who fear progress, will try to give you new and strange names for what we are doing. Sometimes they will call it "Facism," sometimes "Communism," sometimes "Regimentation," sometimes "Socialism." But, in so doing, they are trying to make very complex and theoretical something that is really very simple and very practical.

I believe in practical explanations and in practical policies. I believe that what we are doing today is a necessary fulfillment of what Americans have always been doing—a fulfillment of old and tested American ideals.

Let me give you a simple illustration.

While I am away from Washington this summer, a long-needed renovation of and addition to our White House office building is to be started. The architects have planned a few new rooms built into the present all too small one-story structure. We are going to include in this addition and in this renovation modern electric wiring and modern plumbing and modern means of keeping the offices cool in the hot Washington summers. But the structural lines of the old Executive office building will remain. The artistic lines of the White House Buildings were the creation of master builders when our Republic was young. The simplicity and the strength of the structure remain in the face of every modern test. But within this magnificent pattern, the necessities of modern government business require constant reorganization and rebuilding.

If I were to listen to the arguments of some prophets of calamity who are talking these days, I should hesitate to make these alterations. I should fear that while I am away for a few weeks the architects might build some strange new Gothic tower or a factory building or perhaps a replica of the Kremlin or of the Potsdam Palace. But I have no such fears. The architects and builders are men of common sense and artistic American tastes. They know that the principles of harmony and of necessity itself require that the building of the new structure shall blend with the essential lines of the old. It is this combination of the old and the new that marks orderly peaceful progress, not only in building buildings but in building government itself.

Our new structure is a part of and a fulfillment of the old.

All that we do seeks to fulfill the historic traditions of the American people. Other Nations may sacrifice democracy for the transitory stimulation of old and discredited autocracies. We are restoring confidence and well-being under the rule of the people themselves. We remain, as John Marshall said a century ago, "emphatically and truly, a government of the people." Our Government "in form and in substance . . . emanates from them. Its powers are granted by them, and are to be exercised directly on them, and for their benefits."

Before I close, I want to tell you of the interest and pleasure with which I look forward to the trip on which I hope to start in a few days. It is a good thing for everyone who can possibly do so to get away at least once a year for a change of scene. I do not want to get into the position of not being able to see the forest because of the thickness of the trees.

I hope to visit our fellow Americans in Puerto Rico, in the Virgin Island, in the Canal Zone and in Hawaii. And, incidentally, it will give me an opportunity to exchange a friendly word of greeting with the Presidents of our sister Republics, Haiti and Colombia and Panama.

After four weeks on board ship, I plan to land at a port in our Pacific Northwest, and then will come to the best part of the whole trip, for I am hoping to inspect a number of our new great national projects on the Columbia, Missouri and Mississippi Rivers, to see some of the national parks and, incidentally, to learn much of actual conditions during the trip across the continent back to Washington.

While I was in France during the War our boys used to call the United States "God's country." Let us make it and keep it "God's country."

SECOND INAUGURAL ADDRESS
January 20, 1937

My Fellow Countrymen:

When four years ago we met to inaugurate a President, the Republic, single-minded in anxiety, stood in spirit here. We dedicated ourselves to the fulfillment of a vision—to speed the time when there would be for all the people that security and peace essential to the pursuit of happiness. We of the Republic pledged ourselves to drive from the temple of our ancient faith those who had profaned it; to end by action, tireless and unafraid, the stagnation and despair of that day.

We did those first things first.

Our covenant with ourselves did not stop there. Instinctively we recognized a deeper need—the need to find through government the instrument of our united purpose to solve for the individual the ever-rising problems of a complex civilization.

Repeated attempts at their solution without the aid of government had left us baffled and bewildered. For, without that aid, we had been unable to create those moral controls over the services of science which are necessary to make science a useful servant instead of a ruthless master of mankind. To do this we knew that we must find practical controls over blind economic forces and blindly selfish men.

We of the Republic sensed the truth that democratic government has innate capacity to protec its people against disasters once considered inevitable—to solve problems once considered unsolvable. We would not admit that we could not find a way to master economic epidemics just as, after centuries of fatalistic suffering, we had found a way to master epidemics of disease. We refused to leave the problems of our common welfare to be solved by the winds of chance and the hurricanes of disaster.

In this we Americans were discovering no wholly new truth; we were writing a new chapter in our book of self-government.

This year marks the one hundred and fiftieth anniversary of the constitutional convention which made us a nation. At that convention our forefathers found the way out of the chaos which followed the Revolutionary War; they created a strong government with powers of united action sufficient then and now to solve problems utterly beyond individual or local solution. A century and a half ago they established the Federal Government in order to promote the general welfare and secure the blessings of liberty to the American people.

Today we invoke those same powers of government to achieve the same objectives.

Four years of new experience have not belied our historic instinct. They hold out the clear hope that government within communities, government within the separate States, and government of the United States can do the things the times require, without yielding its democracy. Our tasks in the last four years did not force democracy to take a holiday.

Nearly all of us recognize that as intricacies of human relationships increase, so power to govern them also must increase—power to stop evil; power to do good. The essential democracy of our nation and the safety of our people depend not upon the absence of power but upon lodging it with those whom the people can change or continue at stated intervals through an honest and free system of elections. The Constitution of 1787 did not make our democracy impotent.

In fact, in these last four years, we have made the exercise of all power more democratic; for we have begun to bring private autocratic powers into their proper subordination to the public's government. The legend that they were invincible—above and beyond the processes of a democracy—has been shattered. They have been challenged and beaten.

Our progress out of the depression is obvious.

But that is not all that you and I mean by the new order of things. Our pledge was not merely to do a patchwork job with second-hand materials. By using the new materials of social justice we have undertaken to erect on the old foundations a more enduring structure for the better use of future generations.

In that purpose we have been helped by achievements of mind and spirit. Old truths have been relearned, untruths have been unlearned. We have always known that heedless self-interest was bad morals; we know now that it is bad economics. Out of the collapse of a prosperity whose builders boasted their practicality has come the conviction that in the long run economic morality pays.

We are beginning to wipe out the line that divides the practical from the ideal, and in so doing we are fashioning an instrument of unimagined power for the establishment of a morally better world.

This new understanding undermines the old admiration of worldly success as such. We are beginning to abandon our tolerance of the abuse of power by those who betray for profit the elementary decencies of life.

In this process evil things formerly accepted will not be so easily condoned. Hard-headedness will not so easily excuse hard-heartedness. We are moving toward an era of good feeling. But we realize that there can be no era of good feeling save among men of good-will.

For these reasons I am justified in believing that the greatest change we have witnessed has been the change in the moral climate of America.

Among men of good-will, science and democracy together offer an ever-richer life and ever-larger satisfaction to the individual. With this change in our moral climate and our rediscovered ability to improve our economic order, we have set our feet upon the road of enduring progress.

Shall we pause now and turn our back upon the road that lies ahead? Shall we call this the promised land? Or shall we continue on our way? For "each age is a dream that is dying, or one that is coming to birth."

Many voices are heard as we face a great decision. Comfort says "tarry a while." Opportunism says "This is a good spot." Timidity asks "how difficult is the road ahead?"

True, we have come far from the days of stagnation and despair. Vitality has been preserved. Courage and confidence have been restored. Mental and moral horizons have been extended.

But our present gains were won under the pressure of more than ordinary circumstance. Advance became imperative under the the goad of fear and suffering. The times were on the side of progress.

To hold to progress today, however, is more difficult. Dulled conscience, irresponsibility and ruthless self-interest already reappear. Such symptoms of prosperity may become portents of disaster! Prosperity already tests the persistence of our progressive purpose.

Let us ask again: Have we reached the goal of our vision of that fourth day of March, 1933? Have we found our happy valley?

I see a great nation, upon a great continent, blessed with a great wealth of natural resources. Its hundred and thirty million people are at peace among themselves; they are making their country a good neighbor among the nations. I see a United States which can demonstrate that, under democratic methods of government, national wealth can be translated into a spreading volume of human comforts hitherto unknown—and the lowest standard of living can be raised far above the level of mere subsistence.

But here is the challenge to our democracy: In this nation I see tens of millions of its citizens—a substantial part of its whole population—who at this very moment are denied the greater part of what the very lowest standards of today call the necessities of life.

I see millions of families trying to live on incomes so meager that the pall of family disaster hangs over them day by day.

I see millions whose daily lives in city and on farm continue under conditions labeled indecent by a so-called polite society half a century ago.

I see millions denied education, recreation and the opportunity to better their lot and the lot of their children.

I see millions lacking the means to buy the products of farm and factory and by their poverty denying work and productiveness to many other millions.

I see one-third of a nation ill-housed, ill-clad, ill-nourished.

It is not in despair that I paint you that picture. I paint it for you in hope, because the nation, seeing and understanding the injustice in it, proposes to paint it out. We are determined to make every American citizen the subject of his country's interest and concern, and we will never regard any faithful law-abiding group within our borders as superfluous. The test of our progress is not whether we add more to the abundance of those who have much, it is whether we provide enough for those who have too little.

If I know aught of the spirit and purpose of our nation, we will not listen to comfort, opportunism and timidity. We will carry on.

Overwhelmingly, we of the Republic are men and women of good-will, men and women who have more than warm hearts of dedication, men and women who have cool heads and willing hands of practical purpose as well. They will insist that every agency of popular government use effective instruments to carry out their will.

Government is competent when all who compose it work as trustees for the whole people. It can make constant progress when it keeps abreast of the facts. It can obtain justified support and legitimate criticism when the people receive true information of all that government does.

If I know aught of the will of our people, they will demand that these conditions of effective government shall be created and maintained. They will demand a nation uncorrupted by cancers of injustice and, therefore, strong among the nations in its example of the will to peace.

Today we reconsecrate our country to long cherished ideals in a suddenly changed civilization. In every land there are always at work forces that drive men apart and forces that draw men together. In our personal ambitions we are individualists. But in our seeking for economic and political progress as a nation, we all go up —or else all go down—as one people.

To maintain a democracy of effort requires a vast amount of patience in dealing with differing methods, a vast amount of humility. But out of the confusion of many voices rises an understanding of dominant public need. Then political leadership can voice common ideals, and aid in their realization.

In taking again the oath of office as President of the United States, I assume the solemn obligation of leading the American people forward along the road over which they have chosen to advance.

While this duty rests upon me I shall do my utmost to speak their purpose and to do their will, seeking Divine guidance to help us each and every one to give light to them that sit in darkness and to guide our feet into the way of peace.

MESSAGE TO CONGRESS
May 24, 1937

To the Congress of the United States:
    The time has arrived for us to take further action to extend the frontiers of social progress. Such further action initiated by the legislative branch of the government, administered by the Executive and sustained by the judicial is within the common sense framework and purpose of our Constitution and receives beyond doubt the approval of our electorate.
    The overwhelming majority of our population earns its daily bread either in agriculture or in industry. One-third of our population, the overwhelming majority of which is in agriculture or industry, is ill-nourished, ill-clad and ill-housed.
    The overwhelming majority of this nation has little patience with that small minority which vociferates today that prosperity has returned, that wages are good, that crop prices are high and that government should take a holiday.
    The truth of the matter, of course, is that the exponents of the theory of private initiative as the cure for deep-seated national ills want, in most cases, to improve the lot of mankind. But, well-intentioned as they may be, they fail for four evident reasons—first, they see the problem from the point of view of their own business; second, they see the problem from the point of view of their own locality or region; third, they cannot act unanimously because they have no machinery for agreeing among themselves, and, finally, they have no power to bind the inevitable minority of chislers within their own ranks.
    Though we may go far in admitting that innate decency of this small minority, the whole story of our nation proves that social progress has too often been fought by them. In actual practice it has been effectively advanced only by the passage of laws by State Legislatures or the national Congress.
    Today, you and I are pledged to take further steps to reduce the lag in the purchasing power of industrial workers and to strengthen and stabilize the markets for the farmers' products. The two go hand in hand. Each depends for its effectiveness upon the

other. Both working simultaneously will open new outlets for productive capital.

Our nation so richly endowed with natural resources and with a capable and industrious population should be able to devise ways and means of insuring to all our able-bodied working men and women a fair day's pay for a fair day's work.

A self-supporting and self-respecting democracy can plead in justification for the existence of child labor, no economic reason for chiseling workers' wages or stretching workers' hours.

Enlightened business is learning that competition ought not to cause bad social consequences which inevitably react upon the profits of business itself. All but the hopelessly reactionary will agree that to conserve our primary resources of man power, government must have some control over maximum hours, minimum wages, the evil of child labor and the exploitation of unorganized labor.

Nearly twenty years ago in his dissenting opinion in Hammer vs. Dagenhart, Mr. Justice Holmes expressed his view as to the power of Congress to prohibit the shipment in interstate or foreign commerce of the product of the labor of children in factories below what Congress then deemed to be civilized social standards.

Surely the experience of the last twenty years has only served to reinforce the wisdom and the rightness of his views. And, surely if he was right about the power of the Congress over the work of children in the factories, it is equally right that the Congress has the power over decent wages and hours in those same factories. He said:

"I had thought that the propriety of the exercise of a power admitted to exist in some cases was for the consideration of Congress alone and that this court always had disavowed the right to intrude its judgment upon questions of policy or morals. It is not for this court to pronounce when prohibition is necessary to regulation if it ever may be necessary—to say that it is permissible as against strong drink but not as against the product of ruined lives.

"The act does not meddle with anything belonging to the States. They may regulate their internal affairs and their domestic commerce as they like. But when they seek to send their products across the State line they are no longer within their rights. If there were no Constitution and no Congress their power to cross the line would depend upon their neighbors. Under the Constitution such commerce belongs not to the States but to Congress to regulate. It may carry out its views of public policy whatever indirect effect they may have upon the activities of the States.

"Instead of being encountered by a prohibitive tariff at her boundaries the State encounters the public policy of the United States which it is for Congress to express. The public policy of the United States is shaped with a view to the benefit of the nation as a whole. The national welfare as understood by Congress may require a different attitude within its sphere from that of some self-seeking State. It seems to me entirely constitutional for Congress to enforce its understanding by all the means at its command."

Mr. Justice Brandeis, Mr. Justice Clark and Mr. Justice McKenna agreed. A majority of the Supreme Court, however, decided, 5-4, against Mr. Justice Holmes and laid down a rule of constitutional law which has ever since driven into impractical distinctions and subterfuges all attempts to assert the fundamental power of the national government over interstate commerce.

But although Mr. Justice Holmes spoke for a minority of the Supreme Court he spoke for a majority of the American people.

One of the primary purposes of the formation of our Federal Union was to do away with the trade barriers between the States. To the Congress and not to the States was given the power to regulate commerce among the several States. Congress cannot interfere in local affairs, but when goods pass through the channels of commerce from one State to another they become subject to the power of the Congress and the Congress may exercise that power to recognize and protect the fundamental interests of free labor.

And so to protect the fundamental interests of free labor and a free people we propose that only goods which have been produced under conditions which meet the minimum standards of free labor shall be admitted to interstate commerce. Goods produced under conditions which do not meet rudimentary standards of decency should be regarded as contraband and ought not to be allowed to pollute the channels of interstate trade.

These rudimentary standards will of necessity at the start fall far short of the ideal. Even in the treatment of national problems there are geographical and industrial diversities which practical statesmanship cannot wholly ignore. Backward labor conditions and relatively progressive conditions cannot be completely assimilated and made uniform at one fell swoop without creating economic dislocations.

Practical exigencies suggest the wisdom of distinguishing labor conditions which are clearly oppressive from those which are not as fair or as reasonable as they should be under circumstances prevailing in particular industries. Most fair labor standards as a practical matter require some differentiation between industries and localities. But there are a few rudimentary standards of which we may properly ask general and widespread observance. Failure to observe them must be regarded as socially and economically oppressive and unwarranted under almost any circumstance.

Allowing for a few exceptional trades and permitting longer hours on the payment of time and a half for overtime, it should not be difficult to define a general maximum working week. Allowing for appropriate qualifications and general classifications by administrative action, it should also be possible to put some floor below which the wage ought not to fall.

There should be no difficulty in ruling out the products of the children from any fair market. And there should also be little dispute when it comes to ruling out of the interstate markets products of employers who deny to their workers the right of self-organization and collective bargaining, whether through the fear of labor spies, the bait of company unions, or the use of strike-breakers. The abuses disclosed by the investigations of the Senate must be promptly curbed.

With the establishment of these rudimentary standards as a base we must seek to build up, through appropriate administrative machinery, minimum wage standards of fairness and reasonableness, industry by industry, having due regard to local and geographical diversities and to the effect of unfair labor conditions upon competitors in interstate trade and upon the maintenance of industrial peace.

Although a goodly portion of the goods of American industry move in interstate commerce and will be covered by the legislation which we recommend, there are many purely local pursuits and services which no Federal legislation can effectively cover. No State is justified in sitting idly by and expecting the Federal Government to meet State responsibility for those labor conditions with which the State may effectively deal without fear of unneighborly competition from sister States. The proposed Federal legislation should be a stimulus and not a hindrance to State action.

As we move resolutely to extend the frontiers of social progress, we must be guided by practical reason and not by barren formulae. We must ever bear in mind that our objective is to improve and not to impair the standard of living of those who are now undernourished, poorly clad and ill-housed.

We know that overwork and underpay do not increase the national income when a large portion of our workers remain unemployed. Reasonable and flexible use of the long established right of government to set and to change working hours can, I hope, decrease unemployment in those groups in which unemployment today principally exists.

Our problem is to work out in practice those labor standards which will permit the maximum but prudent employment of our human resources to bring within the reach of the average man and woman a maximum of goods and of service conducive to the fulfillment of the promise of American life.

Legislation can, I hope, be passed at this session of Congress further to help those who toil in factory and on farm. We have promised it. We cannot stand still.

QUARANTINE ADDRESS AT CHICAGO

October 5, 1937

I am glad to come once again to Chicago and especially to have the opportunity of taking part in the dedication of this important project of civic betterment.

On my trip across the continent and back I have been shown many evidences of the result of common-sense cooperation between municipalities and the Federal Government, and I have been greeted by tens of thousands of Americans who have told me in every look and word that their material and spiritual well-being has made great strides forward in the past few years.

And yet, as I have seen with my own eyes the prosperous farms, the thriving factories and the busy railroads—as I have seen the happiness and security and peace which covers our wide land—almost inevitably I have been compelled to contrast our peace with very different scenes being enacted in other parts of the world.

It is because the people of the United States under modern conditions must, for the sake of their own future, give thought to the rest of the world, that I, as the responsible executive head of the nation, have chosen this great inland city and this gala occasion to speak to you on a subject of definite national importance.

The political situation in the world, which of late has been growing progressively worse, is such as to cause grave concern and anxiety to all the peoples and nations who wish to live in peace and amity with their neighbors.

Some nine years ago the hopes of mankind for a continuing era of international peace were raised to great heights when more than sixty nations solemnly pledged themselves not to resort to arms in furtherance of their national aims and policies. The high aspirations expressed in the Briand-Kellogg Peace Pact and the hopes for peace thus raised have of late given way to a haunting fear of calamity.

The present reign of terror and international lawlessness began a few years ago. It began through unjustified interference in the international affairs of other nations or the invasion of alien territory in violations of treaties, and has now reached a stage where the very foundations of civilization are seriously threatened.

The landmarks and traditions which have marked the progress of civilization toward a condition of law, order and justice are being wiped away.

Without a declaration of war and without warning or justification of any kind, civilians, including women and children, are being ruthlessly murdered with bombs from the air.

In times of so-called peace, ships are being attacked and sunk by submarines without cause or notice. Nations are fomenting and taking sides in civil warfare in nations that have never done them any harm. Nations claiming freedom for themselves deny it to others.

Innocent peoples and nations are being cruelly sacrificed to a greed for power and supremacy which is devoid of all sense of justice and humane consideration.

To paraphrase a recent author: "Perhaps we foresee a time when men, exultant in the technique of homicide, will rage so hotly over the world that every precious thing will be in danger, every book and picture and harmony, every treasure garnered through two millenniums, the small, the delicate, the defenseless—all will be lost or wrecked or utterly destroyed."

If those things come to pass in other parts of the world, let no one imagine that America will escape, that it may expect mercy, that this Western Hemisphere will not be attacked and that it will continue tranquilly and peacefully to carry on the ethics and the arts of civilization.

If those days come, "there will be no safety by arms, no help from authority, no answer in science. The storm will rage till every flower of culture is trampled and all human beings are leveled in a vast chaos."

If those days are not to come to pass—if we are to have a world in which we can breathe freely and live in amity without fear—the peace-loving nations must make a concerted effort to uphold laws and principles on which alone peace can rest secure.

The peace-loving nations must make a concerted effort in opposition to those violations of treaties and those ignorings of humane instincts which today are creating a state of international anarchy and instability from which there is no escape through mere isolation or neutrality.

Those who cherish their freedom and recognize and respect the equal right of their neighbors to be free and live in peace must work together for the triumph of law and moral principles in order that peace, justice and confidence may prevail in the world.

There must be a return to a belief in the pledged word, in the value of a signed treaty. There must be recognition of the fact that national morality is as vital as private morality.

A Bishop wrote me the other day:

"It seems to be that something greatly needs to be said in behalf of ordinary humanity against the present practice of carrying the horrors of war to helpless civilians, especially women and children.

"It may be that such a protest might be regarded by many, who claim to be realists, as futile, but may it not be that the heart of mankind is so filled with horror at the present needless suffering that that force could be mobilized in sufficient volume to lessen such cruelty in the days ahead?

"Even though it may take twenty years, which God forbid, for civilization to make effective its corporate protest against this barbarism, surely strong voices may hasten the day."

There is a solidarity and interdependence about the modern world, both technically and morally, which makes it impossible for any nation completely to isolate itself from economic and political upheavals in the rest of the world, especially when such upheavals appear to be spreading and not declining.

There can be no stability or peace either within nations or between nations except under laws and moral standards adhered to by all. International anarchy destroys every foundation for peace. It jeopardizes either the immediate or the future security of every nation, large or small.

It is, therefore, a matter of vital interest and concern to the people of the United States that the sanctity of international treaties and the maintenance of international morality be restored.

The overwhelming majority of the peoples and nations of the world today want to live in peace.

They seek the removal of barriers against trade.

They want to exert themselves in industry, in agriculture and in business that they may increase their wealth through the production of wealth-producing goods rather than striving to produce military planes and bombs and machine guns and cannon for the destruction of human lives and useful property.

In those nations of the world which seem to be piling armament on armament for purposes of aggression, and those other nations which fear acts of aggression against them and their security, a very high proportion of the national income is being spent directly for armaments. It runs from 30 to as high as 50 per cent.

The proportion that we in the United States spend is far less— 11 or 12 per cent.

How happy we are that the circumstances of the moment permit us to put our money into bridges and boulevards, dams and reforestation, the conservation of our soil and many other kinds of useful works, rather than into huge standing armies and vast supplies of implements of war.

I am compelled and you are compelled, nevertheless, to look ahead. The peace, the freedom and the security of 90 per cent of the population of the world is being jeopardized by the remaining 10 per cent who are threatening a breakdown of all international order and law.

Surely the 90 per cent who want to live in peace under law and in accordance with moral standards that have received almost universal acceptance through the centuries, can and must find some way to make their will prevail.

The situation is definitely of universal concern. The questions involved relate not merely to violations of specific provisions of particular treaties; they are questions of war and of peace, of international law, and especially of principles of humanity. It is true that they involve definite violations of agreements, and especially of the Covenant of the League of Nations, the Briand-Kellogg Pact and the Nine-Power Treaty. But they also involve problems of world economy, world security and world humanity.

It is true that the moral consciousness of the world must recognize the importance of removing injustices and well-founded grievances; but at the same time it must be aroused to the cardinal necessity of honoring sanctity of treaties, of respecting the rights and liberties of others and of putting an end to acts of international aggression.

It seems to be unfortunately true that the epidemic of world lawlessness is spreading.

When an epidemic of physical disease starts to spread, the community approves and joins in a quarantine of the patients in order to protect the health of the community against the spread of the disease.

It is my determination to pursue a policy of peace and to adopt every practicable measure to avoid involvement in war.

It ought to be inconceivable that in this modern era, and in the face of experience, any nation could be so foolish and ruthless as to run the risk of plunging the whole world into war by invading and violating, in contravention of solemn treaties, the territory of other nations that have done them no real harm and which are too weak to protect themselves adequately. Yet the peace of the world and the welfare and security of every nation is today being threatened by that very thing.

No nation which refuses to exercise forbearance and to respect the freedom and rights of others can long remain strong and retain the confidence and respect of other nations. No nation ever loses its dignity or good standing by conciliating its differences, and by exercising great patience with, and consideration for, the rights of other nations.

War is a contagion, whether it be declared or undeclared. It can engulf states and peoples remote from the original scene of hostilities. We are determined to keep out of war, yet we cannot insure ourselves against the disastrous effects of war and the dangers of involvement. We are adopting such measures as will minimize our risk of involvement, but we cannot have complete protection in a world of disorder in which confidence and security have broken down.

If civilization is to survive, the principles of the Prince of Peace must be restored. Shattered trust between nations must be revived.

Most important of all, the will for peace on the part of peace-loving nations must express itself to the end that nations that may be tempted to violate their agreements and the rights of others will desist from such a cause. There must be positive endeavors to preserve peace.

America hates war. America hopes for peace. Therefore America actively engages in the search for peace.

MESSAGE TO CONGRESS
November 15, 1937

To the Congress:

Important measures are already pending before this Congress, and other matters will require early consideration. Therefore, it has seemed advisable to call this extraordinary session to expedite the work of the regular session which will begin in January.

Since your adjournment in August there has been a marked recession in industrial production following a fairly steady advance for more than four years.

We have not been unaware of uncertainties in the economic picture. As far back as last Spring I called attention to the rapid rise in many prices—a rise that threatened in particular the anticipated revival of building. And over a month ago I quoted one of the country's leading economists to this effect—that the continuance of business recovery in the United States depends far more upon business policies than it does upon anything that may be done, or not done, in Washington.

The present decline has not reached serious proportions. But it has the effect of decreasing the national income—and that is a matter of definite concern.

During the adjournment of the Congress I have sought to avail myself of the wisdom and advice of managers of large industrial and financial enterprises, of owners of small businesses in many lines, and of representatives of agriculture and of labor.

Out of long experience I place great value on this method of getting suggestions from every possible source. Single answers or simple slogans will not cure the complicated economic problems which today face all nations.

To overemphasize one symptom out of many, to overemphasize any one panacea that for the moment appeals to any one group, is to play with the lives of all the men and women of America.

The ultimate answer to the conditions of today is a cordial and confident cooperation not only between government and every kind of citizen, but also between every kind of citizen and his government. As never before in our history, the well-being of those who have much, as well as those who have less, depends upon a contented society of good-will where the good-will rests on the solid foundation that all have enough.

From these conferences and from other sources many suggestions have come to me and to other members of the executive branch of the government. Some of these recommendations are consistent with each other; some are at complete variance.

But these discussions make it clear that we have enough wisdom in the country today not only to check the present recession but to lay the groundwork for a more permanent recovery. If the people are as willing as government to use the economic knowledge gained in recent years, this recession need go no further.

With the exercise of ordinary prudence, there is no reason why we should suffer any prolonged recession, let alone any general economic paralysis. Despite some maladjustments, which can be corrected, underlying conditions are not unfavorable.

The fundamental situation is not to be compared with the far different conditions of 1929. The banking system is not overextended. Interest rates are lower. Inventories are not dangerously large. We are no longer overextended in new construction or in capital equipment. Speculation requiring liquidation does not overhang our markets.

Obviously an immediate task is to try to increase the use of private capital to create employment. Private enterprise, with cooperation on the part of government, can advance to higher levels of industrial activity than those reached earlier this year. Such advance will assure balanced budgets. But obviously, also, government cannot let nature take its course without regard to consequences. If private enterprise does not respond, government must take up the slack.

What we can do covers so wide a field and so many subjects that it is not feasible to include them all in this message.

A little later I will address you further in regard to proposals to encourage private capital to enter the field of new housing on a large scale—a field which during the past four years has failed almost completely to keep pace with the marked improvement in other industries.

On the subject of taxation, in accordance with my suggestion of last Spring, committees of the Congress, with the cooperation of the Treasury Department, are already engaged in studies aimed at the elimination of any injustices in our tax laws. Unjust provisions should be removed, provided such removal does not create new injustices.

Modifications adequate to encourage productive enterprise, especially for the smaller businesses, must not extend to the point of using the corporate form for the purpose of hiding behind it to reduce or eliminate taxes in a way not open to an individual or partnership.

Nor should we extend tax privileges to speculative profits on capital where the intent of the original risk was speculation rather than the actual development of productive enterprise. Nor can we at this time accept a revision of our revenue laws which involves a reduction in the aggregate revenues or an increase in the aggregate tax burdens of those least able to bear them.

We should give special consideration to lightening inequitable burdens on the enterprise of the small business men of the nation. Small businesses or even those of average size have difficulties of financing and distribution which are not shared by large corporations. Therefore, by special tax consideration they should receive more equal opportunity to compete with their more powerful competitors.

In this way we may also find assistance in our search for a more effective method of checking the growing concentration of economic control and the resultant monopolistic practices which persist today in spite of anti-trust statutes. A further search for additional methods to meet this threat to free competitive enterprise is called for at this time.

The proposed Federal budget for the coming fiscal year also will shortly be ready for submission to the Congress—a budget which I expect can be brought within a definite balance.

Still other matters are receiving renewed examination—for instance the problems of the railroads and of other public utilities. Here because of thoroughly unsound financing extending over many past years, solutions will frankly be difficult.

But as we work with these problems of detail we must not forget the broad central truth that this administration has pledged itself to the people of the United States to carry on with a wide social program pointed toward higher living standards and a more just distribution of the gains of civilization. Much of that program is already in effect, but its continued and complete success depends on a wider distribution of an immensely enlarged national income. Such enlargement presupposes full employment of both capital and labor—reasonable profits and fair wages—a resumption of that vigorous moving equilibrium which began in 1933. Deflation and inflation are equal enemies of the balanced economy that will produce that progressive increase in national income.

In the attainment of the broad central purpose we recognize many related objectives. This message, however, deals with only four of these objectives—four which are already being considered by the Congress. Two relate directly to the stabilization and maintenance of the purchasing power of the nation. The other two, essential tools for the whole task, look to the improvement of the machinery and functioning of both the executive and legislative branches of the Federal Government.

1. AGRICULTURE

Intention to pass a new and permanent national farm act was declared by the Congress in joint resolution last Summer. Great as the need was then, that need is still greater today. Some crops will begin to be planted within three months.

In recent weeks farmers have once more been facing acute surpluses and falling prices. Cotton farmers are harvesting the largest cotton crop in all our history—5,000,000 bales more than the markets of this country and of the world have been accustomed to take. Corn farmers and potato farmers are harvesting crops that threaten to crush them for producing this plenty. And the producers of other crops are wondering how soon they, too, will be the victims of surplus uncontrolled.

We must continue in our efforts toward abundance without waste. We need legislation which will not only prevent new farm surpluses from causing new collapse in farm prices but which will also safeguard farmers and consumers against the hazards of crop failure. We need an "all weather" farm plan—a plan that uses the reasonable surpluses of a year of good weather to carry over food supplies to make up for the shortages of a year of bad weather.

Out of the experience of the last five years we have learned that with the aid of the government, farmers can successfully guard themselves against economic disaster.

In formulating a farm program there are certain things we must keep in mind.

We must keep in mind the fertility of our soil. We have begun to assist farmers to stop the waste of soil and save the good soil that remains. Any sound, long-time program must have soil conservation as a principal goal.

We must keep in mind the economic welfare of farm families. As a long-time national policy, farmers must have a fair share in the national income to supply farmers' buying to keep city factories running.

We must keep in mind the consumers of the nation. The blighting droughts of 1934 and 1936, which spelled disaster for so many farmers in those years, were brought forcibly home to our large cities in the high prices of many foodstuffs this year. Consumers should have the same protection against the underproduction of years of scarcity as the farmers should have against the overproduction of years of glut.

We must keep in mind the American democratic way. Farm programs cannot long succeed unless they have the active support of the farmers who take part in them. Our program should continue to be one planned and administered, so far as possible, by the farmers themselves. Here again majority rules seems justified. If and when huge surpluses in any one crop threaten to engulf all the producers of that crop, our laws should provide ways by which a small minority may be kept from destroying the proceeds of the toil of the great majority.

We must keep in mind the United States Treasury. I have already expressed my view that if the new farm act provides for expenditure of funds beyond those planned in the regular budget, additional means should be provided to yield the additional revenue. May I reiterate that with all the emphasis I can give?

We must keep in mind the Constitution of the United States. Although vital portions of the Agricultural Adjustment Act were set aside nearly two years ago by the Supreme Court, acts of Congress to improve labor relations and assure workers' security have since then been upheld. In these later decisions the powers of the Federal Government to regulate commerce between the States and to tax and to spend for the general welfare have been closely recognized.

I believe that the courts themselves are coming to have increasing regard for the true nature of the Constitution as a broad charter of democratic government which can function under the conditions of today. I believe that the Congress can constitutionally write an adequate farm act that will be well within the broad meaning and purpose of the Constitution.

I hope and believe that the Supreme Court will not again deny to farmers the protection which it now accords to others.

2. LABOR

I believe that the country as a whole recognizes the need for immediate Congressional action if we are to maintain wage income and the purchasing power of the nation against recessive factors in the general industrial situation. The exploitation of child labor and the undercutting of wages and the stretching of the hours of the poorest paid workers in periods of business recession has a serious effect on buying power. In the interest of the national economy such adjustments as must be made should not be made at the expense of those least able to bear them.

I further believe that the country as a whole realizes the necessary connection between encouraging business men to make capital expenditures for new plants and raising the total wage income of the total of our working population. New plants today mean labor-saving machinery. What does the country ultimately gain if we encourage business men to enlarge the capacity of American industry to produce, unless we see to it that the income of our working population actually expands sufficiently to create markets to absorb that increased production?

I further believe that the country as a whole recognizes the need of seeking a more uniformly adequate standard of living and purchasing power everywhere, if every part is to live happily with every other part. We do not recognize the destiny of any State or any county to be permanently backward. Political and social harmony requires that every State and every county not only produce goods for the nation's markets but furnish markets for the nation's goods.

This does not mean that legislation must require immediate uniform minimum hour or wage standards; that is an ultimate goal.

We should provide flexible machinery which will enable industries throughout the country to adjust themselves progressively to better labor conditions. But we must not forget that no policy of flexibility will be practical unless a coordinating agency has the obligation of inspection and investigation to ensure the recognition and enforcement of what the law requires.

Although there are geographical and industrial diversities which practical statesmanship cannot well ignore, it is high time that we we had legislation relating to goods moving in or competing with interstate commerce which will accomplish two immediate purposes:

First. Banish child labor and protect workers unable to protect themselves from excessively low wages and excessively long hours.

Second. End the unsound practice of some communities—by no means confined to any one section of the country—which seek new industries by offering as the principal attraction labor more plentiful and much cheaper than may be found in competing communities. To them the Congress should reiterate the oft-repeated pledge of political parties that labor is not a mere commodity.

3. ORGANIZATION

Last January I presented for the consideration of the Congress the improvement of administrative management in the executive branch of the government. Five principal objectives were outlined:

(a) To create one or more additional departments and to give the Chief Executive authority to arrange all present and future strictly executive activities in or under regular executive departments.

(b) To establish a budget and efficiency agency, a personnel agency and a planning agency through which the Chief Executive may coordinate the executive functions.

(c) To permit the Chief Executive to make a slight increase in the White House staff so that he may keep in close touch with, and maintain knowledge of, the widespread affairs of administration which require his final direction.

(d) To establish accountability of the Executive to the Congress by providing a genuine independent audit by an officer solely responsible to the Congress, who will, however, have no administrative part in the transactions he audits and certifies.

(e) To extend the merit system upward, outward and downward to cover practically all non-policy determining posts. I am giving consideration to proposed executive orders extending the merit principle of selection under the authority vested in me by the Constitution and revised statutes.

Executive orders, however, have not the permanence of law; they will not lessen the need for permanent legislation on this subject in connection with reorganization. I, therefore, seek a statutory modernized machinery for the permanent enforcement of merit principles in appointment, promotion and personnel management throughout the government service.

The experience of States and municipalities definitely proves that reorganization of government along the lines of modern business administrative practice can increase efficiency, minimize error, duplication and waste, and raise the morale of the public service. But that experience does not prove, and no person conversant with the management of large private corporations or of governments honestly suggests, that reorganization of government machinery in the interest of efficiency is a method of making major savings in the cost of government.

Large savings in the cost of government can be made only by cutting down or eliminating government functions. And to those who advocate such a course, it is fair to put the question—Which functions of government do you advocate cutting off?

4. PLANNING

Of equal importance with intelligent reorganization of the executive departments is intelligent reorganization of our methods of spending national funds for the conservation and development of those natural resources which are the foundation of a virile national life. I said in a special message to the Congress last Spring, We have reached a stage in the depletion of our national resources where we should allot a definite portion of each year's budget to this work of husbandry.

Our present machinery for carrying out such purposes, however, is geared to methods of which the rivers-and-harbors legislation of many years ago is an example. We spend sporadically—on a project here and a project there, determined upon without relation to the needs of other localities—without relation to possibly more important needs of the same locality—without relation to the national employment situation or the Federal budget.

To avoid waste and to give the nation its money's worth from the national funds we expend, we must, like any business corporation, have a definite building and operating plan worked out ahead of time—a planned order in which to make expenditures, a planned timing for expenditures so that we may keep our working force employed, and a planned coordinated use of the projects after completion.

And because relative values of local projects should be appraised before they come to Washington, first by those with local knowledge and then by regional conferences, we must have some kind of local and regional planning machinery and coordination to get full value out of the final appropriations authorized in Washington—money value and human value.

Last year I recommended such machinery. For this purpose of conservation and development of our natural resources, I recommended that the country be divided into the seven great regions into which nature divided those resources—that in such regions local authorities be set up to arrange projects into some kind of comprehensive and continuing plan for the entire region—and that only after such consideration should regional projects be submitted to the Executive and to the Congress for inclusion in a national development program of such size as the budget of the year will permit.

Such machinery will provide decentralization. It will give local communities and the nation alike new confidence in the true worth of such expenditures.

What these four subjects promise in continued and increased purchasing power—what they promise in greater efficiency in the use of government funds—are intelligent foundations for the other plans for encouragement of industrial expansion with government help. What they promise in social contentment is an almost necessary basis for greater security of profits and property.

In the months they have been before the Congress they have been discussed from one end of the country to the other.

For the sake of the nation, I hope for your early action.

ADDRESS AT THOUSAND ISLAND BRIDGE

August 18, 1938

Mr. Prime Minister, it has always seemed to me that the best symbol of common sense was a bridge. Common sense is sometimes slow in getting into action, and perhaps this is why we took so long to build this one.

It is a particular pleasure to me to meet you here, where a boundary is a gateway and not a wall. Between these islands an international gap, never wide, has been spanned, as gaps usually are, by the exercise of ability, guided by cooperative common sense. I hope all our countrymen will use it freely. I know they will find, as I have done, a happy welcome on either shore, and for the right fellowship from neighbors who are also friends.

The St. Lawrence River is more than a cartographic line between our two countries. God so formed North America that the waters of an inland empire drain into the Great Lakes basin. The rain which falls in this vast area finds outlet through this single natural funnel, above which we now stand.

Events of history have made that river a boundary, and as a result the flow of these waters can be used only by joint agreement between our two governments. Between us, we stand, therefore, as trustees for two countries of one of the richest natural assets provided anywhere in the world. The water which runs underneath this bridge spells unlimited power; permits access to raw materials both from this Continent and from beyond the seas, and enhances commerce and production.

When a resource of this kind is placed at our very doors, I think the plain people of both countries agree that it is ordinary common sense to make use of it. Yet up to now the liquid wealth, which flowing water is, has run in large part unused to the sea.

I really think that this situation suggests that we can agree upon some better arrangement than merely letting it contribute a miscroscopic fraction to the level of the North Atlantic Ocean.

The bridge which we here dedicate is a tangible proof that administration by two neighbors of a job to be done in common offers no difficulty. Obviously the same process applied on the larger scale to the resource of full seagoing navigation and of complete power development offered by the St. Lawrence River can build and maintain the necessary facilities to employ its magnificent possibilities.

I suppose it is true, as has been true of all natural resources, that a good many people would like to have the job—and the profits —of developing it for themselves. In this case, however, the river happens to be placed in the hands of our two governments, and the responsibility for getting the results lies plainly at our doors.

At various times both the people of Canada and the people of the United States have dreamed of the St. Lawrence and Great Lakes development. They have translated those ideas into plans which can easily be carried out.

While there has been no difference between us as to the object, history compels me to say that we were not able to arrange matters so that both peoples have had the same idea at the same time. How would it do for a change, if, instead of each of having the idea at alternate intervals, we get the idea simultaneously. I think we are rapidly reaching that happy and desirable event.

I am very clear that prophets of trouble are wrong when they express the fear that the St. Lawrence waterway will handicap our railroad systems. We know now that the effect of a waterway is not to take traffic away from railroad lines. Actually, it creates new possibilities, new businesses, new activity. Such a waterway generates more railroad traffic than it takes away.

There is today a fourteen-foot channel carrying traffic from the Great Lakes through the St. Lawrence River into the Atlantic Ocean. If this were deepened—which can easily be done—to twenty-seven or thirty feet, every city on the Great Lakes, now inland, would become an ocean port.

The banks of the St. Lawrence Valley would become one of the great gateways of the world and would benefit accordingly. Here all that is needed is cooperative exercise of technical skill by joint use of the imagination and the vision which our two countries have.

Can any one doubt that, when this is done, the interests of both countries will be greatly advanced? Do we need to delay, and to deprive our peoples of the immediate employment and profit, or prevent our generation from reaping the harvest which is awaiting us?

Let me make, now, an unusual statement. I am sure you will not misunderstand. I consider that I have, myself, a particular duty in connection with St. Lawrence power. The almost unparalleled opportunity which the river affords has not gone unnoticed by some of my friends on our side of the boundary. A conception has been emerging in the United States which is not without a certain magnificence. This is no less than the conviction that if a private group could control the outlet of the Great Lakes basin, that group would have a monopoly in the development of a territory larger than many of the great empires in history.

If you were to search the records with which my government is familiar, you would discover that literally every development of electric power, save only the Ontario-Hydro, is allied to, if not controlled by, a single American group, with, of course, the usual surrounding penumbra of allies, affiliates, subsidiaries and satellites.

In earlier states of development of natural resources on this continent, this was normal and usual. In recent decades, however, we have come to realize the implications to the public—to the individual men and women, to business men, big and little, and even to government itself, resulting from the ownership by any group of the right to dispose of wealth which was granted to us collectively by nature herself.

The development of natural resources, and the proper handling of their fruits, is a major problem of government. Naturally, no solution would be acceptable to either country which does not leave its government entirely master in its own house.

To put it bluntly, a group of American interests is here gradually putting itself into a position where, unless caution is exercised, they may in time be able to determine the economic fate of a large area, both in Canada and the United States.

Now, it is axiomatic in Canadian-American relations that both of us scrupulously respect the right of each to determine its own affairs.

For that reason, when I know that the operation of uncontrolled American economic forces is slowly producing a result on the Canadian side of the border which I know very well must eventually give American groups a great influence over Canadian development, I consider it the part of a good neighbor to discuss the question frankly. The least I can do is to call attention to the situation as I see it.

Our mutual friendship suggests this course in a matter of development as great and as crucial as that of the St. Lawrence. Fortunately among friendly nations today this is increasingly being done. Frank discussion between friends and neighbors is useful and essential. It is obvious today that some economic problems are international, if only because of the sheer weight which the solutions have on the lives of people, as well as inside any one country. To my mind, the development of St. Lawrence navigation and power is such a problem.

I look forward to the day when a Canadian Prime Minister and an American President can meet to dedicate, not a bridge across this water, but the very water itself, to the lasting and productive use of their respective peoples. Until that day comes, and I hope it may be soon, this bridge stands as an open door. There will be no challenge at the border, and no guard to ask a countersign. Where the boundary is crossed the only word must be, "pass, friend."

President Franklin D. Roosevelt speaking at his first inaugural March 4, 1933

HARRIS AND EWING PHOTO

May 7, 1933   HARRIS AND EWING PHOTO
President Roosevelt broadcasts his second Fireside Chat to the nation.

HARRIS AND EWING PHOTO

President Roosevelt delivering his 2nd Inaugural Address while thousands of hardy citizens listened despite the heavy downpour. Vice President Garner and Chief Justice Hughes can be seen in the picture, January 20, 1937.

On June 1, 1940 at Commencement Exercises at the University of Virginia, President Roosevelt denounced Mussolini and declared ". . . the hand that held the dagger has struck it in the back of its neighbor." These words electrified the audience which applauded wildly.

HARRIS AND EWING PHOTO

President Roosevelt was roundly cheered by the huge crowd which listened to his speech on the occasion of his taking the oath of office for the third time. (January 20, 1941)

HARRIS AND EWING PHOTO

HARRIS AND EWING PHOTO

On September 11, 1941 in an address to the nation from the White House President Roosevelt said that as a result of the attempted torpedoing of the U. S. S. Greer, German and Italian vessels entering the waters on this side of the Atlantic, will do so at their own peril.

HARRIS AND EWING PHOTO

With a world map as a backdrop, President Roosevelt here in a Radio Address from the White House reported to the American people the progress of the great struggle which they had to fight and how the results of battles fought thousands of miles away effected even the remotest towns in this country. The President is pointing to the Pacific area. (February 23, 1942)

HARRIS AND EWING PHOTO

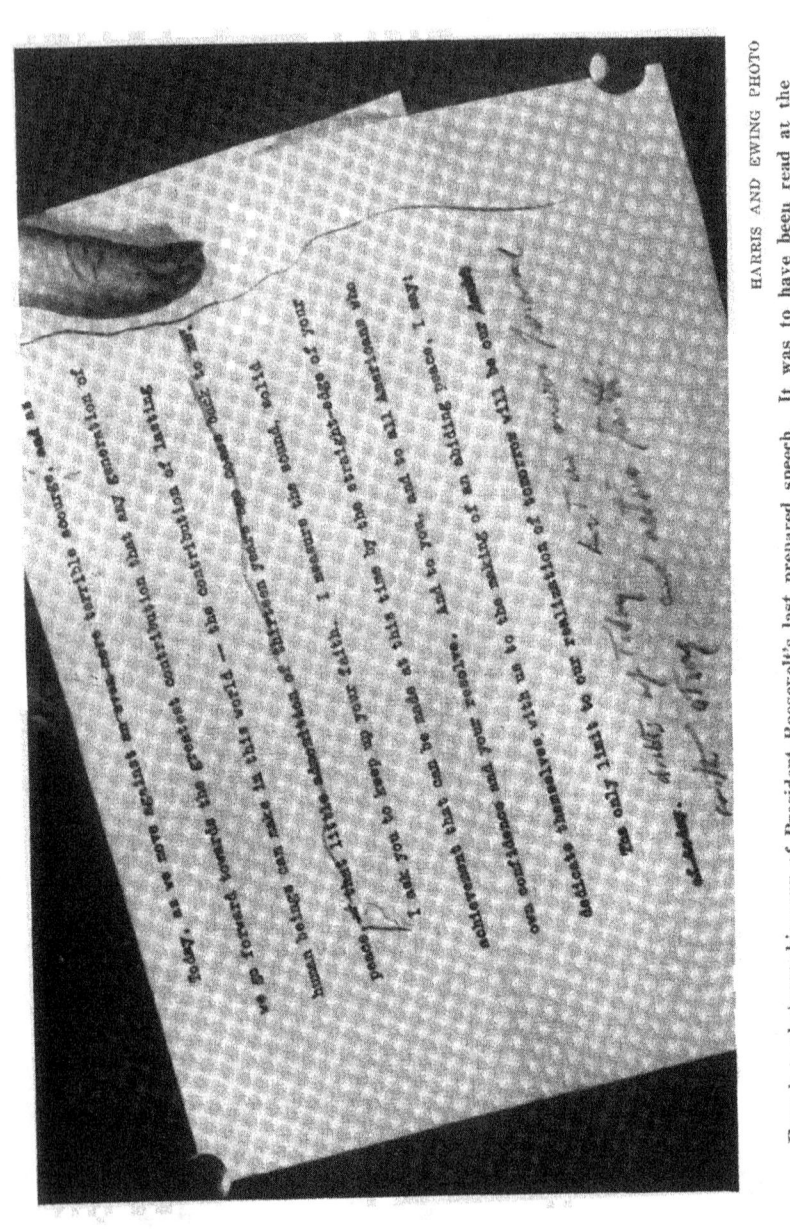

Here is a photographic copy of President Roosevelt's last prepared speech. It was to have been read at the Jefferson Day Dinner in Washington on Friday April 13th, 1945. Corrections had been made by the President and he has penciled in a last sentence.

TALK AT QUEEN'S UNIVERSITY

August 18, 1938

To the pleasure of being once more on Canadian soil, where I have passed so many of the happy hours of my life, there is added today a very warm sense of gratitude for being admitted to the fellowship of this ancient and famous university. I am glad to join the brotherhood which Queens has contributed and is contributing not only to the spiritual leadership for which the college was established, but also to the social and public leadership in the civilized life of Canada.

An American President is precluded by our Constitution from accepting any title from a foreign prince, potentate or power. Queen's University is not a prince or a potentate but it is a power. Yet I can say, without constitutional reserve, that the acceptance of the title which you confer on me today would raise no qualms in the august breast of our own Supreme Court.

Civilization is not national—it is international—even though that observation—trite to most of us, is today challenged in some parts of the world. Ideas are not limited by territorial borders; they are the common inheritance of all free people. Thought is not anchored in any land; and the profit of education rebounds to the equal benefit of the whole world. That is one form of free trade to which the leaders of every opposing political party can subscribe.

In a large sense we in the Americas stand charged today with the maintaining of that tradition. When, speaking recently in a similar vein in the Republic of Brazil, I included the Dominion of Canada in the fellowship of the Americas, our South American neighbors gave hearty acclaim. We in the Americas know the sorrow and the wreckage which may follow if the ability of men to understand each other is rooted out from among the nations.

Many of us here today know from experience that of all the devastations of war none is more tragic than the destruction which it brings to the process of men's minds. Truth is denied because emotion pushes it aside. Forebearance is succeeded by bitterness. In that atmosphere human thought cannot advance.

It is impossible not to remember that for years when Canadians and Americans have met they have light-heartedly saluted as North American friends, without thought of dangers from overseas. Yet we are awake to knowledge that the casual assumptions of our greetings in earlier times today must become a matter for serious thought.

A few days ago, a whisper, fortunately untrue, raced round the world that armies standing over against each other in unhappy array were to be set in motion. In a few short hours the effect of that whisper had been registered in Montreal and New York, in Ottawa and in Washington, in Toronto and in Chicago, in Vancouver and in San Francisco. Your business men and ours felt it alike; your farmers and ours heard it alike; your young men and ours wondered what effect this might have on their lives.

We in the Americas are no longer a far away continent, to which the eddies of controversies beyond the seas have become a consideration to every general staff beyond the seas. The vast amount of our resources, the vigor of our commerce and the strength of our men have made us vital factors in world peace whether we choose or not.

Happily, you and we, in friendship and in entire understanding, can look clear-eyed at these possibilities, resolving to leave no pathway unexplored and no technique undeveloped which may, if our hopes are realized, contribute to the peace of the world. Even if those hopes are disappointed, we can assure each other that this hemisphere at least shall remain a strong citadel wherein civilization can flourish unimpaired.

The Dominion of Canada is part of the sisterhood of the British Empire. I give to you assurance that the people of the United States will not stand idly by if domination of Canadian soil is threatened by any other empire.

We are good neighbors and true friends because we maintain our own rights with frankness, because we refuse to accept the twists of secret diplomacy, because we settle our disputes by consultation and because we discuss our common problems in the spirit of the common good.

We seek to be scrupulously fair and helpful not only in our relations with each other but each of us at home in our relations with our own people.

But there is one process which we certainly cannot change and probably ought not to change. This is the feeling which ordinary men and women have about events which they can understand. We cannot prevent our people from having an opinion in regard to wanton brutality, in regard to undemocratic regimentation, in regard to misery inflicted on helpless peoples, or in regard to violations of accepted individual rights.

All that any government, constituted as is yours and mine, can possibly undertake is to help make sure that the facts are known and fairly stated. No country where thought is free can prevent every fireside and home within its borders from considering the evidence for itself and rendering its own verdict; and the sum total of these conclusions of educated men and women will, in the long run, become the national verdict.

That is what we mean when we say that public opinion ultimately governs policy. It is right and just that this should be the case.

Many of our ancestors came to Canada and the United States because they wished to break away from systems which forbade them to think freely and their descendants have insisted on the right to know the truth—to argue their problems to a majority decision, and, if they remained unconvinced, to disagree in peace. As a tribute to our likeness in that respect, I note that the Bill of Rights in your country and in mine is substantially the same.

Mr. Chancellor, you of Canada who respect the educational tradition of our democratic continent will ever maintain good neighborship in ideas as we in the public service hope and propose to maintain it in the field of government and of foreign relations. My good friend, the Governor General, in receiving an honorary degree in June at that university of Cambridge, Mass., to which Mackenzie King and I both belong, suggested that we cultivate three qualities to keep our foothold in the shifting sands of the present—humility, humanity and humor. All three of them, imbedded in education, build new spans to re-establish free intercourse throughout the world and bring forth an order in which free nations can live in peace.

ADDRESS AT CHARLOTTESVILLE
"*The Dagger in the Back*"
June 10, 1940

President Newcomb, my friends of the University of Virginia.

I notice by the program that I am asked to address the classes of 1940. I avail myself of that privilege, but I also take this very happy occasion to speak to many other classes—classes that have graduated through all the years, classes that are still in the period of study, classes not alone of the schools of learning of the nation, but classes that have come up through the great schools of experience. In other words, a cross-section, a cross-section just as you who graduate today are a cross-section of the nation as a whole.

Every generation of young men and women in America has questions to ask the world. Most of the time they are the simple but nevertheless difficult questions—questions of work to do, opportunities to find, ambitions to satisfy.

But every now and again in the history of the republic a different kind of question presents itself—a question that asks, not about the future of an individual or even of a generation, but about the future of the country, the future of the American people.

There was such a time at the beginning of our history, at the beginning of our history as a nation. Young people asked themselves in those days what lay ahead, not for themselves, but for the new United States.

There was such a time again in the seemingly endless years of the war between the States. Young men and young women on both sides of the line asked themselves, not what trades or professions they would enter, what lives they would make, but what was to become of the country they had known.

There *is* such a time again today. Again today the young men and the young women of America ask themselves with earnestness and with deep concern this same question: "What is to become of the country we know?"

Now they ask it with even greater anxiety than before. They ask, not only what the future holds for this republic, but what the future holds for all peoples and all nations that have been living under democratic forms of government—under the free institutions of a free people.

It is understandable to all of us, I think, that they should ask this question. They read the words of those who are telling them that the ideal of individual liberty, the ideal of free franchise, the ideal of peace through justice is a decadent ideal.

They read the word and hear the boast of those who say that a belief in force—force directed by self-chosen leaders—is the new and vigorous system which will overrun the earth. They have seen the ascendency of this philosophy of force in nation after nation where free institutions and individual liberties were once maintained.

It is natural and understandable that the younger generation should first ask itself what the extension of the philosophy of force to all the world would lead to ultimately. We see today, for example, in stark reality some of the consequences of what we call the machine age.

Where control of machines has been retained in the hands of mankind as a whole, untotaled benefits have accrued to mankind. For mankind was then the master: The machine was the servant.

But in this new system of force the mastery of the machine is not in the hands of mankind. It is in the control of infinitely small groups of individuals who rule without a single one of the democratic sanctions that we have known.

The machine in the hands of irresponsible conquerors becomes the master; mankind is not only the servant, it is the victim too. Such mastery abandons with deliberate contempt all of the moral values to which even this young country for more than 300 years has been accustomed and dedicated.

Surely the new philosophy proves from month to month that it could have no possible conception of the way of life or the way of thought of a nation whose origins go back to Jamestown and Plymouth Rock.

And conversely, neither those who spring from that ancient stock nor those who have come hither in later years can be indifferent to the destruction of freedom in their ancestral lands across the sea.

Perception of danger to our institutions may come slowly or it may come with a rush and shock as it has to the people of the United States in the past few months. This perception of danger—danger in a world-wide arena—has come to us clearly and overwhelmingly. We perceive the peril in this world-wide arena—an arena that may become so narrow that only the Americas will retain the ancient faiths.

Some indeed still hold to the now somewhat obvious delusion that we of the United States can safely permit the United States to become a lone island, a lone island in a world dominated by the philosophy of force.

Such an island may be the dream of those who still talk and vote as isolationists. Such an island represents to me and to the overwhelming majority of Americans today a helpless nightmare, the helpless nightmare of a people without freedom. Yes, the nightmare of a people lodged in prison, handcuffed, hungry and fed through the bars from day to day by the contemptuous, unpitying masters of other continents.

It is natural also that we should ask ourselves how now we can prevent the building of that prison and the placing of ourselves in the midst of it.

Let us not hesitate—all of us—to proclaim certain truths. Overwhelmingly we, as a nation, and this applies to all the other American nations, we are convinced that military and naval victory for the gods of force and hate would endanger the institutions of democracy in the Western World—and that equally, therefore, the whole of our sympathies lie with those nations that are giving their life blood in combat against those forces.

The people and Government of the United States have seen with the utmost regret and with grave disquiet the decision of the Italian Government to engage in the hostilities now raging in Europe.

More than three months ago the chief of the Italian Government sent me word that because of the determination of Italy to limit, so far as might be possible, the spread of the European conflict, more than two hundred millions of people in the region of the Mediterranean had been enabled to escape the suffering and the devastation of war.

I informed the chief of the Italian Government that this desire on the part of Italy to prevent the war from spreading met with full sympathy and response on the part of the government and the people of the United States, and I expressed the earnest hope of this government and of this people that this policy on the part of Italy might be continued. I made it clear that in the opinion of the Government of the United States any extension of hostilities in the region of the Mediterranean might result in the still greater enlargement of the scene of the conflict, the conflict in the Near East and in Africa, and that if this came to pass no one could foretell how much greater the theatre of war eventually might become.

Again, upon a subsequent occasion, not so far ago, recognizing that certain aspirations of Italy might form the basis of discussions between the powers most specifically concerned, I offered, in a message addressed to the chief of the Italian Government, to send to the Governments of France and Great Britain such specific indi-

"Dagger in the Back" 65

cations of the desires of Italy to obtain readjustments with regard to her position as the chief of the Italian Government might desire to transmit through me.

While making it clear that the government of the United States in such an event could not and would not assume responsibility for the nature of the proposals submitted nor for agreements which might thereafter be reached, I proposed that if Italy would refrain from entering the war I would be willing to ask assurances from the other powers concerned that they would faithfully execute any agreement so reached, and that Italy's voice in any future peace conference would have the same authority as if Italy had actually taken part in the war as a belligerent.

Unfortunately, unfortunately to the regret of all of us, and to the regret of humanity, the chief of the Italian Government was unwilling to accept the procedure suggested, and he has made no counter-proposal. This government directed its efforts to doing what it could to work for the preservation of peace in the Mediterranean area, and it likewise expressed its willingness to endeavor to cooperate with the government of Italy when the appropriate occasion arose for the creation of a more stable world order, through the reduction of armaments and through the construction of a more liberal international economic system which would assure to all powers equality of opportunity in the world markets and in the securing of raw materials on equal terms.

I have likewise, of course, felt it necessary in my communications to Signor Mussolini to express the concern of the government of the United States because of the fact that any extension of the war in the region of the Mediterranean would inevitably result in great prejudice to the ways of life and government and to the trade and commerce of all the American republics.

The government of Italy has now chosen to preserve what it terms its "freedom of action" and to fulfill what it states are its promises to Germany. In so doing it has manifested disregard for the rights and security of other nations, disregard for the lives of the peoples of those nations which are directly threatened by the spread of this war; and has evinced its unwillingness to find the means through Pacific negotiations for the satisfaction of what it believes are its legitimate aspirations.

On this 10th day of June, 1940, the hand that held the dagger has struck it into the back of its neighbor.

On this 10th day of June, 1940, in this university founded by the first great American teacher of democracy, we send forth our prayers and our hopes to those beyond the seas who are maintaining with magnificent valor their battle for freedom.

In our unity, in our American unity, we will pursue two obvious and simultaneous courses; we will extend to the opponents of force the material resources of this nation and, at the same time, we will harness and speed up the use of those resources in order that we ourselves in the Americas may have equipment and training equal to the task of any emergency and every defense.

All roads leading to the accomplishment of these objectives must be kept clear of obstructions. We will not slow down or detour. Signs and signals call for speed—full speed ahead.

Yes, it is right that each new generation should ask questions. But in recent months the principal question has been somewhat simplified. Once more the future of the nation and the future of the American people is at stake.

We need not and we will not, in any way, abandon our continuing efforts to make democracy work within our borders. Yes, we still insist on the need for vast improvements in our own social and economic life.

But that, that is a component part of national defense itself.

The program unfolds swiftly and into that program will fit the responsibility and the opportunity of every man and woman in the land to preserve our heritage in days of peril.

I call for effort, courage, sacrifice, devotion. Granting the love of freedom, all of these are possible.

And the love of freedom is still fierce, still steady in the nation today.

CALL FOR FULL RESPONSE ON DEFENSE
December 29, 1940

My Friends:

This is not a fireside chat on war. It is a talk on national security; because the nub of the whole purpose of your President is to keep you now, and your children later, and your grandchildren much later, out of a last-ditch war for the preservation of American independence and all of the things that American independence means to you and to me and to ours.

Tonight, in the presence of a world crisis, my mind goes back eight years to a night in the midst of a domestic crisis. It was a time when the wheels of American industry were grinding to a full stop, when the whole banking system of our country had ceased to function.

I well remember that while I sat in my study in the White House, preparing to talk with the people of the United States, I had before my eyes the picture of all those Americans with whom I was talking. I saw the workmen in the mills, the mines, the factories; the girl behind the counter; the small shopkeeper; the farmer doing his Spring plowing; the widows and the old men wondering about their life's savings.

I tried to convey to the great mass of American people what the banking crisis meant to them in their daily lives.

Tonight I want to do the same thing, with the same people, in this new crisis which faces America.

We met the issue in 1933 with courage and realism. We face this new crisis—this new threat to the security of our nation—with the same courage and realism.

Never before since Jamestown and Plymouth Rock has our American civilization been in such danger as now.

For on September 27, 1940—this year—by an agreement signed in Berlin, three powerful nations, two in Europe and one in Asia, joined themselves together in the threat that if the United States of America interferred with or blocked the expansion program of these three nations—a program aimed at world control—they would unite in ultimate action against the United States.

The Nazi masters of Germany have made it clear that they intend not only to dominate all life and thought in their own country, but also to enslave the whole of Europe, and then to use the resources of Europe to dominate the rest of the world.

It was only three weeks ago that their leader stated this: "There are two worlds that stand opposed to each other." And then in defiant reply to his opponents he said this: "Others are correct when they say: 'With this world we cannot ever reconcile ourselves.' * * * I can beat any other power in the world." So said the leader of the Nazis.

In other words, the Axis not merely admits but the Axis proclaims that there can be no ultimate peace between their philosophy —their philosophy of government—and our philosophy of government.

In view of the nature of this undeniable threat, it can be asserted, properly and categorically, that the United States had no right or reason to encourage talk of peace until the day shall come when there is a clear intention on the part of the aggressor nations to abandon all thought of dominating or conquering the world.

At this moment the forces of the States that are leagued against all peoples who live in freedom are being held away from our shores. The Germans and the Italians are being blocked on the other side of the Atlantic by the British and by the Greeks, and by thousands of soldiers and sailors who were able to escape from subjugated countries. In Asia the Japanese are being engaged by the Chinese nation in another great defense.

In the Pacific Ocean is our fleet.

Some of our people like to believe that wars in Europe and Asia are of no concern to us. But it is a matter of most vital concern to us that European and Asiatic war-makers should not gain control of the oceans which lead to this hemisphere.

One hundred and seventeen years ago the Monroe Doctrine was conceived by our government as a measure of defense in the face of a threat against this hemisphere by an alliance in Continental Europe. Thereafter, we stood guard in the Atlantic, with the British as neighbors. There was no treaty. There was no "unwritten agreement."

And yet there was the feeling, proven correct by history, that we as neighbors could settle any disputes in peaceful fashion. And the fact is that during the whole of this time the Western Hemisphere has remained free from agression from Europe or from Asia.

Does any one seriously believe that we need to fear attack anywhere in the Americas while a free Britain remains our most powerful naval neighbor in the Atlantic? And does any one seriously believe, on the other hand, that we could rest easy if the Axis powers were our neighbors there?

If Great Britain goes down, the Axis powers will control the Continents of Europe, Asia, Africa, Australia, and the high seas—and they will be in a position to bring enormous military and naval resources against this hemisphere. It is no exaggeration to say that all of us in all the Americas would be living at the point of a gun—a gun loaded with explosive bullets, economic as well as military.

We should enter upon a new and terrible era in which the whole world, our hemisphere included, would be run by threats of brute force. And to survive in such a world, we would have to convert ourselves permanently into a militaristic power on the basis of war economy.

Some of us like to believe that even if Britain falls, we are still safe, because of the broad expanse of the Atlantic and of the Pacific.

But the width of those oceans is not what it was in the days of clipper ships. At one point between Africa and Brazil the distance is less than it is from Washington to Denver, Colo., five hours for the latest type of bomber. And at the north end of the Pacific Ocean, America and Asia almost touch each other.

Why, even today we have planes that could fly from the British Isles to New England and back again without refueling. And remember that the range of the modern bomber is being ever increased.

During the past week many people in all parts of the nation have told me what they wanted me to say tonight. Almost all of them expressed a courageous desire to hear the plain truth about the gravity of the situation. One telegram, however, expressed the attitude of the small minority who want to see no evil and hear no evil, even though they know in their hearts that evil exists. That telegram begged me not to tell again of the ease with which our American cities could be bombed by any hostile power which had gained bases in this Western Hemisphere. The gist of that telegram was: "Please, Mr. President, don't frighten us by telling us the facts."

Frankly and definitely there is danger ahead—danger against which we must prepare. But we well know that we cannot escape danger, or the fear of danger, by crawling into bed and pulling the covers over our heads.

Some nations of Europe were bound by solemn non-intervention pacts with Germany. Other nations were assured by Germany that they need never fear invasion. Non-intervention pact or not, the fact remains that they were attacked, overrun, thrown into modern slavery at an hour's notice or even without any notice at all.

As an exiled leader of one of these nations said to me the other day, "The notice was a minus quantity. It was given to my government two hours after German troops had poured into my country in a hundred places." The fate of these nations tells us what it means to live at the point of a Nazi gun.

The Nazis have justified such actions by various pious frauds. One of these frauds is the claim that they are occupying a nation for the purpose of "restoring order." Another is that they are occupying or controlling a nation on the excuse that they are "protecting it" against the aggression of somebody else.

For example, Germany has said that she was occupying Belgium to save the Belgians from the British. Would she then hesitate to say to any South American country: "We are occupying you to protect you from aggression by the United States?"

Belgium today is being used as an invasion base against Britain, now fighting for its life. And any South American country, in Nazi hands, would always constitute a jumping off place for German attack on any one of the other republics of this hemisphere.

Analyze for yourselves the future of two other places even nearer to Germany if the Nazis won. Could Ireland hold out? Would Irish freedom be permitted as an amazing pet exception in an unfree world? Or the islands of the Azores, which still fly the flag of Portugal after five centuries? You and I think of Hawaii as an outpost of defense in the Pacific. And yet the Azores are closer to our shores in the Atlantic than Hawaii is on the other side.

There are those who say that the Axis powers would never have any desire to attack the Western Hemisphere. That is the same dangerous form of wishful thinking which has destroyed the powers of resistance of so many conquered peoples. The plain facts are that the Nazis have proclaimed, time and again, that all other races are their inferiors and therefore subject to their orders. And most important of all, the vast resources and wealth of this American hemisphere constitute the most tempting loot in all of the round world.

Let us no longer blind ourselves to the undeniable fact that the evil forces which have crushed and undermined and corrupted so many others are already within our own gates. Your government knows much about them and every day is ferreting them out.

Their secret emissaries are active in our own and in neighboring countries. They seek to stir up suspicion and dissension, to cause internal strife. They try to turn capital against labor, and vice versa. They try to reawaken long slumbering racial and religious enmities which should have no place in this country. They are active in every group that promotes intolerance. They exploit for their own ends our own natural abhorrence of war.

These trouble-breeders have but one purpose. It is to divide our people, to divide them into hostile groups and to destroy our unity and shatter our will to defend ourselves.

There are also American citizens, many of them in high places, who, unwittingly in most cases, are aiding and abetting the work of these agents. I do not charge these American citizens with being foreign agents. But I do charge them with doing exactly the kind of work that the dictators want done in the United States.

These people not only believe that we can save our own skins by shutting our eyes to the fate of other nations. Some of them go much further than that. They say that we can and should become the friends and even the partners of the Axis powers. Some of them even suggest that we should imitate the methods of the dictatorships. But Americans never can and never will do that.

The experience of the past two years has proven beyond doubt that no nation can appease the Nazis. No man can tame a tiger into a kitten by stroking it. There can be no appeasement with ruthlessness. There can be no reasoning with an incendiary bomb. We know now that a nation can have peace with the Nazis only at the price of total surrender.

Even the people of Italy have been forced to become accomplices of the Nazis; but at this moment they do not know how soon they will be embraced to death by their allies.

The American appeasers ignore the warning to be found in the fate of Austria, Czecho-Slovakia, Poland, Norway, Belgium, the Netherlands, Denmark and France. They tell you that the Axis powers are going to win anyway; that all of this bloodshed in the world could be saved, that the United States might just as well throw its influence into the scale of a dictated peace and get the best out of it that we can.

They call it a "negotiated peace." Nonsense! Is it a negotiated peace if a gang of outlaws surrounds your community and on threat of extermination makes you pay tribute to save your own skins?

Such a dictated peace would be no peace at all. It would be only another armistice, leading to the most gigantic armament race and the most devastating trade wars in all history. And in these contests the Americas would offer the only real resistance to the Axis powers. With all their vaunted efficiency, with all their parade of pious purpose in this war, there are still in their background the concentration camp and the servants of God in chains.

The history of recent years proves that the shootings and the chains and the concentration camps are not simply the transient tools but the very altars of modern dictatorships. They may talk of a "new order" in the world, but what they have in mind is only a revival of the oldest and worst tyranny. In that there is no liberty, no religion, no hope.

The proposed "new order" is the very opposite of a United States of Europe or a United States of Asia. It is not a government based upon the consent of the governed. It is not a union of ordinary, self-respecting men and women to protect themselves and their freedom and their dignity from oppression. It is an unholy alliance of power and pelf to dominate and enslave the human race.

The British people and their allies today are conducting an active war against this unholy alliance. Our own future security is greatly dependent on the outcome of that fight. Our ability to "keep out of war" is going to be affected by that outcome.

Thinking in terms of today and tomorrow, I make the direct statement to the American people that there is far less chance of the United States getting into war if we do all we can now to support the nations defending themselves against attack by the Axis than if we acquiesce in their defeat, submit tamely to an Axis victory, and wait our turn to be the object of attack in another war later on.

If we are to be completely honest with ourselves, we must admit that there is risk in any course we may take. But I deeply believe that the great majority of our people agree that the course that I advocate involves the least risk now and the greatest hope for world peace in the future.

The people of Europe who are defending themselves do not ask us to do their fighting. They ask us for the implements of war, the planes, the tanks, the guns, the freighters which will enable them to fight for their liberty and for our security. Emphatically we must get these weapons to them, get them to them in sufficient volume and quickly enough so that we and our children will be saved the agony and suffering of war which others have had to endure.

Let not the defeatists tell us that it is too late. It will never be earlier. Tomorrow will be later than today.

Certain facts are self-evident.

In a military sense Great Britain and the British Empire are today the spearhead of resistance to world conquest. And they are putting up a fight which will live forever in the story of human gallantry.

There is no demand for sending an American expeditionary force outside our own borders. There is not intention by any member of your government to send such a force. You can, therefore, nail, nail any talk about sending armies to Europe as deliberate untruth.

Our national policy is not directed toward war. Its sole purpose is to keep war away from our country and away from our people.

Democracy's fight against world conquest is being greatly aided, and must be more greatly aided, by the rearmament of the United States and by sending every ounce and every ton of munitions and supplies that we can possibly spare to help the defenders who are in the front lines. And it is no more unneutral for us to do that than it is for Sweden, Russia and other nations near Germany to send steel and ore and oil and other materials into Germany every day in the week.

We are planning our own defense with the utmost urgency, and in its vast scale we must integrate the war needs of Britain and the other free nations which are resisting aggression.

This is not a matter of sentiment or of controversial personal opinion. It is a matter of realistic, practical military policy, based on the advice of our military experts who are in close touch with existing warfare. These military and naval experts and the members of the Congress and the Administration have a single-minded purpose—the defense of the United States.

This nation is making a great effort to produce everything that is necessary in this emergency—and with all possible speed. And this great effort requires great sacrifice.

I would ask no one to defend a democracy which in turn would not defend every one in the nation against want and privation. The strength of this nation shall not be diluted by the failure of the government to protect the economic well-being of its citizens.

If our capacity to produce is limited by machines, it must ever be remembered that these machines are operated by the skill and the stamina of the workers. As the government is determined to protect the rights of the workers, so the nation has a right to expect that the men who man the machines will discharge their full responsibilities to the urgent needs of defense.

The worker possesses the same human dignity and is entitled to the same security of position as the engineer or the manager or the owner. For the workers provide the human power that turns out the destroyers, and the planes and the tanks.

The nation expects our defense industries to continue operation without interruption by strikes or lockouts. It expects and insists that management and workers will reconcile their differences by voluntary or legal means, to continue to produce the supplies that are so sorely needed.

And on the economic side of our great defense program, we are, as you know, bending every effort to maintain stability of prices and with that the stability of the cost of living.

Nine days ago I announced the setting up of a more effective organization to direct our gigantic efforts to increase the production of munitions. The appropriation of vast sums of money and a well-coordinated executive direction of our defense efforts are not in themselves enough. Guns, planes, ships and many other things have to be built in the factories and the arsenals of America. They have to be produced by workers and managers and engineers with the aid of machines which in turn have to be built by hundreds of thousands of workers throughout the land.

In this great work there has been splendid cooperation between the government and industry and labor. And I am very thankful.

American industrial genius, unmatched throughout all the world in the solution of production problems, has been called upon to bring its resources and its talents into action. Manufacturers of watches, of farm implements, of linotypes and cash registers and automobiles, and sewing machines and lawn mowers and locomotives, are now making fuses and bomb packing crates and telescope mounts and shells and pistols and tanks.

But all of our present efforts are not enough. We must have more ships, more guns, more planes—more of everything. And this can be accomplished only if we discard the notion of "business as usual." This job cannot be done merely by super-imposing on the existing productive facilities the added requirements of the nation for defense.

Our defense efforts must not be blocked by those who fear the future consequences of surplus plant capacity. The possible consequences of failure of our defense efforts now are much more to be feared.

And after the present needs of our defense are past, a proper handling of the country's peacetime needs will require all of the new productive capacity, if not still more.

No pessimistic policy about the future of America shall delay the immediate expansion of those industries essential to defense. We need them.

I want to make it clear that it is the purpose of the nation to build now with all possible speed every machine, every arsenal, every factory that we need to manufacture our defense material. We have the men—the skill—the wealth—and above all, the will.

I am confident that if and when production of consumer or luxury goods in certain industries requires the use of machines and raw materials that are essential for defense purposes, then such production must yield, and will gladly yield, to our primary and compelling purpose.

So I appeal to the owners of plants—to the managers—to the workers—to our own government employes—to put every ounce of effort into producing these munitions swiftly and without stint. With this appeal I give you the pledge that all of us who are officers of your government will devote ourselves to the same whole-hearted extent to the great task that lies ahead.

As planes and ships and guns and shells are produced, your government, with its defense experts, can then determine how best to use them to defend this hemisphere. The decision as to how much shall be sent abroad and how much shall remain at home must be made on the basis of our over-all military necessities.

We must be the great arsenal of democracy. For us this is an emergency as serious as war itself. We must apply ourselves to our task with the same resolution, the same sense of urgency, the same spirit of patriotism and sacrifice as we would show were we at war.

We have furnished the British great material support and we will furnish far more in the future.

There will be no "bottlenecks" in our determination to aid Great Britain. No dictator, no combination of dictators, will weaken that determination by threats of how they will construe that determination.

The British have received invaluable military support from the heroic Greek army and from the forces of all the governments in exile. Their strength is growing. It is the strength of men and women who value their freedom more highly than they value their lives.

I believe that the Axis powers are not going to win this war. I base that belief on the latest and best of information.

We have no excuse for defeatism. We have every good reason for hope—hope for peace, yes, and hope for the defense of our civilization and for the building of a better civilization in the future.

I have the profound conviction that the American people are now determined to put forth a mightier effort than they have ever yet made to increase our production of all the implements of defense, to meet the threat of our democratic faith.

As President of the United States, I call for that national effort. I call for it in the name of this nation which we love and honor and which we are privileged and proud to serve. I call upon our people with absolute confidence that our common cause will greatly succeed.

MESSAGE TO CONGRESS
January 6, 1941

Mr. Speaker, members of the 77th Congress:

I address you, the members of this new Congress, at a moment unprecedented in the history of the union. I use the word "unprecedented" because at no previous time has American security been as seriously threatened from without as it is today.

Since the permanent formation of our government under the Constitution in 1789, most of the periods of crisis in our history have related to our domestic affairs. And, fortunately, only one of these —the four-year war between the States—ever threatened our national unity. Today, thank God, 130,000,000 Americans in forty-eight States have forgotten points of the compass in our national unity.

It is true that prior to 1914 the United States often has been disturbed by events in other continents. We have been engaged in two wars with European nations and in a number of undeclared wars in the West Indies, in the Mediterranean and in the Pacific, for the maintenance of American rights and for the principles of peaceful commerce. But in no case had a serious threat been raised against our national safety or our continued independence.

What I seek to convey is the historic truth that the United States as a nation has at all times maintained opposition—clear, definite opposition—to any attempt to lock us in behind an ancient Chinese wall while the procession of civilization went past. Today, thinking of our children and of their children, we oppose enforced isolation for ourselves or for any other part of the Americas.

That determination of ours, extending over all these years, was proved, for example, in the early days during the quarter century of wars following the French Revolution.

While the Napoleonic struggle did threaten interests of the United States because of the French foothold in the West Indies and in Louisiana, and while we engaged in the War of 1812 to vindicate our right to peaceful trade, it is nevertheless clear that neither France nor Great Britain nor any other nation was aiming at domination of the whole world.

And in like fashion, from 1815 to 1914—ninety-nine years—no single war in Europe or in Asia constituted a real threat against our future or against the future of any other American nation.

Except in the Maximilian interlude in Mexico, no foreign power sought to establish itself in this hemisphere. And the strength of the British fleet in the Atlantic has been a friendly strength; it is still a friendly strength.

Even when the World War broke out in 1914 it seemed to contain only a small threat of danger to our own American future. But as time went on, as we remember, the American people began to visualize what the downfall of democratic nations might mean to our own democracy.

We need not overemphasize imperfections in the peace of Versailles. We need not harp on failure of the democracies to deal with problems of world reconstruction. We should remember that the peace of 1919 was far less unjust than the kind of pacification which began even before Munich, and which is being carried on under the new order of tyranny that seeks to spread over every continent today.

The American people have unalterably set their faces against that tyranny.

I suppose that every realist knows that the democratic way of life is at this moment being directly assailed in every part of the world—assailed either by arms or by secret spreading of poisonous propaganda by those who seek to destroy unity and promote discords in nations that are still at peace.

During sixteen long months this assault has blotted out the whole pattern of democratic life in an appalling number of independent nations, great and small. And the assailants are still on the march, threatening other nations, great and small.

Therefore, as your President, performing my constitutional duty to "give to the Congress information of the state of the union," I find it unhappily necessary to report that the future and the safety of our country and of our democracy are overwhelmingly involved in events far beyond our borders.

Armed defense of democratic existence is now being gallantly waged in four continents. If that defense fails, all the population and all the resources of Europe and Asia, Africa and Australia will be dominated by conquerors. And let us remember that the total of those populations in those four continents, the total of those populations and their resources greatly exceeds the sum total of the population and the resources of the whole of the Western Hemisphere—yes, many times over.

In times like these it is immature—and, incidentally, untrue—for anybody to brag that an unprepared America, single-handed and with one hand tied behind its back, can hold off the whole world.

No realistic American can expect from a dictator's peace international generosity, or return to true independence, or world disarmament, or freedom of expression, or freedom of religion—or even good business. Such a peace would bring no security for us or for our neighbors. Those who would give up essential liberty to purchase a little temporary safety deserve neither liberty nor safety.

As a nation we may take pride in the fact that we are softhearted; but we cannot afford to be soft-headed. We must always be wary of those who with sounding brass and a tinkling cymbal preach the ism of appeasement. We must especially beware of that small group of selfish men who would clip the wings of the American eagle to feather their own nests.

I have recently pointed out how quickly the tempo of modern warfare could bring into our very midst the physical attack which we must eventually expect if the dictator nations win this war.

There is much loose talk of our immunity from immediate and direct invasion from across the seas. Obviously, as long as the British Navy retains its power, no such danger exists. Even if there were no British Navy it is not probable that any enemy would be stupid enough to attack us by landing troops in the United States from across thousands of miles of ocean, until it had acquired strategic bases from which to operate.

But we learn much from the lessons of the past years in Europe—particularly the lesson of Norway, whose essential seaports were captured by treachery and surprise built up over a series of years.

The first phase of the invasion of this hemisphere would not be the landing of regular troops. The necessary strategic points would be occupied by secret agents and by their dupes—and great numbers of them are already here and in Latin America.

As long as the aggressor nations maintain the offensive they, not we, will choose the time and the place, and the method of their attack.

And that is why the future of all the American Republics is today in serious danger. That is why this annual message to the Congress is unique in our history. That is why every member of the executive branch of the government and every member of the Congress face great responsibility—great accountability.

The need of the moment is that our actions and our policy should be devoted primarily—almost exclusively—to meeting this foreign peril. For all our domestic problems are now a part of the great emergency.

Just as our national policy in internal affairs has been based upon a decent respect for the rights and the dignity of all of our fellow men within our gates, so our national policy in foreign affairs has been based on a decent respect for the rights and the dignity of all nations, large and small. And the justice of morality must and will win in the end.

Our national policy is this:

First, by an impressive expression of the public will and without regard to partisanship, we are committed to all-inclusive national defense.

Second, by an impressive expression of the public will and without regard to partisanship, we are committed to full support of all those resolute people everywhere who are resisting aggression and are thereby keeping war away from our hemisphere. By this support we express our determination that the democratic cause shall prevail, and we strengthen the defense and the security of our own nation.

Third, by an impressive expression of the public will and without regard to partisanship, we are committed to the proposition that principles of morality and considerations for our own security will never permit us to acquiesce in a peace dictated by aggressors and sponsored by appeasers. We know that enduring peace cannot be bought at the cost of other people's freedom.

In the recent national election there was no substantial difference between the two great parties in respect to that national policy. No issue was fought out on this line before the American electorate. And today it is abundantly evident that American citizens everywhere are demanding and supporting speedy and complete action in recognition of obvious danger.

Therefore, the immediate need is a swift and driving increase in our armament production. Leaders of industry and labor have responded to our summons. Goals of speed have been set. In some cases these goals are being reached ahead of time. In some cases we are on schedule; in other cases there are slight but not serious delays. And in some cases—and, I am sorry to say, very important cases—we are still concerned by the slowness of the accomplishment of our plans.

The Army and Navy, however, have made substantial progress during the past year. Actual experience is improving and speeding up our methods of production with every passing day. And today's best is not good enough for tomorrow.

I am not satisfied with the progress thus far made. The men in charge of the program represent the best in training, in ability and in patriotism. They are not satisfied with the progress thus far made. None of us will be satisfied until the job is done.

No matter whether the original goal was set too high or too low, our objective is quicker and better results.

To give you two illustrations:

We are behind schedule in turning out finished airplanes. We are working day and night to solve the innumerable problems and to catch up.

We are ahead of schedule in building warships, but we are working to get even further ahead of that schedule.

To change a whole nation from a basis of peacetime production of implements of peace to a basis of wartime production of implements of war is no small task. The greatest difficulty comes at the beginning of the program, when new tools, new plant facilities, new assembly lines, new shipways must first be constructed before the actual material begins to flow steadily and speedily from them.

The Congress, of course, must rightly keep itself informed at all times of the progress of the program. However, there is certain information, as the Congress itself will readily recognize, which, in the interests of our own security and those of the nations that we are supporting, must of needs be kept in confidence.

New circumstances are constantly begetting new needs for our safety. I shall ask this Congress for greatly increased new appropriations and authorizations to carry on what we have begun.

I also ask this Congress for authority and for funds sufficient to manufacture additional munitions and war supplies of many kinds, to be turned over to those nations which are now in actual war with aggressor nations. Our most useful and immediate role is to act as an arsenal for them as well as for ourselves. They do not need manpower, but they do need billions of dollars' worth of the weapons of defense.

The time is near when they will not be able to pay for them all in ready cash. We cannot, and we will not, tell them that they must surrender merely because of present inability to pay for the weapons which we know they must have.

I do not recommend that we make them a loan of dollars with which to pay for these weapons—a loan to be repaid in dollars. I recommend that we make it possible for those nations to continue to obtain war materials in the United States, fitting their orders into our own program. And nearly all of their material would, if the time ever came, be useful in our own defense.

For what we send abroad we shall be repaid, repaid within a reasonable time following the close of hostilities, repaid in similar materials, or at our option in other goods of many kinds which they can produce and which we need.

Let us say to the democracies:

We Americans are vitally concerned in your defense of freedom. We are putting forth our energies, our resources and our organizing powers to give you the strength to regain and maintain a free world. We shall send you in ever-increasing numbers, ships, planes, tanks, guns. That is our purpose and our pledge.

In fulfillment of this purpose we will not be intimidated by the threats of dictators that they will regard as a breach of international law or as an act of war our aid to the democracies which dare to resist their aggression. Such aid is not an act of war, even if a dictator should unilaterally proclaim it so to be.

And when the dictators—if the dictators—are ready to make war upon us, they will not wait for an act of war on our part.

They did not wait for Norway or Belgium or the Netherlands to commit an act of war. Their only interest is in a new one-way international law which lacks mutuality in its observances and therefore becomes an instrument of oppression. The happiness of future generations of Americans may well depend on how effective and how immediate we can make our aid felt. No one can tell the exact character of the emergency situations that we may be called upon to meet. The nation's hands must not be tied when the nation's life is in danger.

Yes, and we must prepare, all of us prepare, to make the sacrifices that the emergency—almost as serious as war itself—demands. Whatever stands in the way of speed and efficiency in defense, in defense preparations at any time, must give way to the national need.

A free nation has the right to expect full co-operation from all groups. A free nation has the right to look to the leaders of business, of labor and of agriculture to take the lead in stimulating effort, not among other groups but within their own groups.

The best way of dealing with the few slackers or troubemakers in our midst is, first, to shame them by patriotic example, and if that fails, to use the sovereignty of government to save government.

As men do not live by bread alone, they do not fight by armament alone. Those who man our defenses and those behind them who build our defenses must have the stamina and the courage which come from unshakable belief in the manner of life which they are defending. The mighty action that we are calling for cannot be based on a disregard for all the things worth fighting for.

The nation takes great satisfaction and much strength from the things which have been done to make its people conscious of their individual stakes in the preservation of democratic life in America. Those things have toughened the fiber of our people, have renewed their faith and strengthened their devotion to the institutions we make ready to protect.

Certainly this is no time for any of us to stop thinking about the social and economic problems which are the root cause of the social revolution which is today a supreme factor in the world. For there is nothing mysterious about the foundations of a healthy and strong democracy.

The basic things expected by our people of their political and economic systems are simple. They are:

Equality of opportunity for youth and for others.
Jobs for those who can work.
Security for those who need it.
The ending of special privilege for the few.
The preservation of civil liberties for all.
The employment of the fruits of scientific progress in a wider and constantly rising standard of living.

These are the simple, the basic things that must never be lost sight of in the turmoil and unbelievable complexity of our modern world. The inner and abiding strength of our economic and political systems is dependent upon the degree to which they fulfill these expectations.

Many subjects connected with our social economy call for immediate improvement. As examples:

We should bring more citizens under the coverage of old-age pension and unemployment insurance.

We should widen the opportunities for adequate medical care.

We should plan a better system by which persons deserving or needing gainful employment may obtain it.

I have called for personal sacrifice, and I am assured of the willingness of almost all Americans to respond to that call. A part of the sacrifice means the payment of more money in taxes. In my budget message I will recommend that a greater portion of this great defense program be paid for from taxation than we are paying for today. No person should try, or be allowed to get rich out of the program, and the principle of tax payments in accordance with ability to pay should be constantly before our eyes to guide our legislation.

If the Congress maintains these principles the voters, putting patriotism ahead of pocketbooks, will give you their applause.

In the future days which we seek to make secure, we look forward to a world founded upon four essential human freedoms.

The first is freedom of speech and expression—everywhere in the world.

The second is freedom of every person to worship God in his own way—everywhere in the world.

The third is freedom from want, which, translated into world terms, means economic understanding which will secure to every nation a healthy peacetime life for its inhabitants—everywhere in the world.

The fourth is freedom from fear, which, translated into world terms means a world-wide reduction of armaments to such a point and in such a thorough fashion that no nation will be in a position to commit an act of physical aggression against any neighbor—anywhere in the world.

That is no vision of a distant millenium. It is a definite basis for a kind of world attainable in our own time and generation. That kind of world is the very antithesis of the so-called "new order" of tyranny which the dictators seek to create with the crash of a bomb.

To that new order we oppose the greater conception—the moral order. A good society is able to face schemes of world domination and foreign revolutions alike without fear.

Since the beginning of our American history we have been engaged in change, in a perpetual, peaceful revolution, a revolution which goes on steadily, quietly, adjusting itself to changing conditions without the concentration camp or the quicklime in the ditch. The world order which we seek is the co-operation of free countries, working together in a friendly, civilized society.

This nation has placed its destiny in the hands, heads and hearts of its millions of free men and women, and its faith in freedom under the guidance of God. Freedom means the supremacy of human rights everywhere. Our support goes to those who struggle to gain those rights and keep them. Our strength is our unity of purpose.

To that high concept there can be no end save victory.

THIRD INAUGURAL ADDRESS
January 20, 1941

Mr. Chief Justice, my friends:

On each national day of inauguration since 1789 the people have renewed their sense of dedication to the United States.

In Washington's day the task of the people was to create and weld together a nation.

In Lincoln's day the task of the people was to preserve that nation from disruption from within.

In this day the task of the people is to save that nation and its institutions from disruption from without.

To us there has come a time, in the midst of swift happenings, to pause for a moment and take stock—to recall what our place in history has been, and to rediscover what we are and what we may be. If we do not, we risk the real peril of isolation, the real peril of inaction.

Lives of nations are determined not by the count of years, but by the lifetime of the human spirit. The life of a man is threescore years and ten; a little more, a little less. The life of a nation is the fullness of the measure of its will to live.

There are men who doubt this. There are men who believe that democracy, as a form of government and a frame of life, is limited or measured by a kind of mystical and artificial fate—that, for some unexplained reason, tyranny and slavery have become the surging wave of the future, and that freedom is an ebbing tide.

But we Americans know that this is not true.

Eight years ago, when the life of this Republic seemed frozen by a fatalistic terror, we proved that this is not true. We were in the midst of shock; but we acted, we acted quickly, boldly, decisively.

These later years have been living years—fruitful years for the people of this democracy. For they have brought to us greater security and, I hope, a better understanding that life's ideals are to be measured in other than material things.

Most vital to our present and to our future is this experience of a democracy which successfully survived crisis at home; put away many evil things; built new structures on enduring lines; and, through it all, maintained the fact of its democracy.

For action has been taken within the three-way framework of the Constitution of the United States. The co-ordinate branches of the government continue freely to function. The Bill of Rights remains inviolate. The freedom of elections is wholly maintained. Prophets of the downfall of American democracy have seen their dire predictions come to naught.

No, democracy is not dying.

We know it because we have seen it revive and grow.

We know it cannot die, because it is built on the unhampered initiative of individual men and women joined together in a common enterprise—an enterprise undertaken and carried through by the free expression of a free majority.

We konw it because democracy alone, of all forms of government, enlists the full force of men's enlightened will.

We know it because democracy alone has constructed an unlimited civilization capable of infinite progress in the improvement of human life.

We know it because, if we look below the surface, we sense it still spreading on every continent; for it is the most humane, the most advanced, and in the end the most unconquerable of all forms of human society.

A nation, like a person, has a body—a body that must be fed and clothed and housed, invigorated and rested, in a manner that measures up to the standards of our time.

A nation, like a person, has a mind—a mind that must be kept informed and alert, that must know itself, that understands the hopes and the needs of its neighbors—all the other nations that live within the narrowing circle of the world.

A nation, like a person, has something deeper, something more permanent, something larger than the sum of all its parts. It is that something which matters most to its future, which calls forth the most sacred guarding of its present.

It is a thing for which we find it difficult—even impossible—to hit upon a single, simple word.

And yet we all understand what it is—the spirit—the faith of America. It is the product of centuries. It was born in the multitudes of those who came from many lands—some of high degree, but mostly plain people—who sought here, early and late, to find freedom more freely.

The democratic aspiration is no mere recent phase in human history. It is human history. It permeated the ancient life of early peoples. It blazed anew in the Middle Ages. It was written in Magna Carta.

In the Americas its impact has been irresistible. America has been the new world in all tongues, and to all peoples, not because this continent was a new-found land, but because all who came here believed they could create upon this continent a new life—a life that should be new in freedom.

Its vitality was written into our Mayflower Compact, into the Declaration of Independence, into the Constitution of the United States, into the Gettysburg Address.

Those who first came here to carry out the longings of their spirit and the millions who followed, and the stock that sprang from them—all have moved forward constantly and consistently toward an ideal which in itself has gained stature and clarity with each generation.

The hopes of the Republic cannot forever tolerate either undeserved poverty or self-serving wealth.

We know that we still have far to go; that we must more greatly build the security and the opportunity and the knowledge of every citizen, in the measure justified by the resources and the capacity of the land.

But it is not enough to achieve these purposes alone. It is not enough to clothe and feed the body of this nation, to instruct, to inform its mind. For there is also the spirit. And of the three, the greatest is the spirit.

Without the body and the mind, as all men know, the nation could not live. But if the spirit of America were killed, even though the nation's body and mind, constricted in an alien world, lived on, the America we know would have perished.

That spirit—that faith—speaks to us in our daily lives in ways often unnoticed, because they seem so obvious. It speaks to us here in the capital of the nation. It speaks to us through the processes of governing in the sovereignties of forty-eight States. It speaks to us in our counties, in our cities, in our towns, and in our villages. It speaks to us from the other nations of the hemisphere, and from those across the seas—the enslaved, as well as the free.

Sometimes we fail to hear or heed these voices of freedom because to us the privilege of our freedom is such an old, old story.

The destiny of America was proclaimed in words of prophecy spoken by our first President in his inaugural in 1789—words almost directed, it would seem, to this year of 1941: "The preservation of the sacred fire of liberty and the destiny of the republican model of government are justly considered * * * deeply, * * * finally, staked on the experiment intrusted to the hands of the American people."

If you and I, if we in this later day, lose that sacred fire—if we let it be smothered with doubt and fear—then we shall reject the destiny which Washington strove so valiantly and so triumphantly to establish. The preservation of the spirit and faith of the nation does, and will, furnish the highest justification for every sacrifice that we may make in the cause of national defense.

In the face of great perils never before encountered, our strong purpose is to protect and to perpetuate the integrity of democracy.

For this we muster the spirit of America, and the faith of America.

We do not retreat. We are not content to stand still. As Americans, we go forward, in the service of our country, by the will of God.

SPEECH ON GERMAN SUBMARINE ATTACKS
September 11, 1941

My fellow-Americans:
The Navy Department of the United States has reported to me that on the morning of Sept. 4 the United States destroyer Greer, proceeding in full daylight toward Iceland, had reached a point southeast of Greenland. She was carrying American mail to Iceland. She was flying the American flag. Her identity as an American ship was unmistakable.

She was then and there attacked by a submarine. Germany admits that it was a German submarine. The submarine deliberately fired a torpedo at the Greer, followed later by another torpedo attack. In spite of what Hitler's propaganda bureau has invented, and in spite of what any American obstructionist organization may prefer to believe, I tell you the blunt fact that the German submarine fired first upon this American destroyer without warning, and with deliberate design to sink her.

Our destroyer, at the time, was in waters which the Government of the United States had declared to be waters of self-defense, surrounding outposts of American protection in the Atlantic.

In the north of the Atlantic, outposts have been established by us in Iceland, in Greenland, in Laborator and in Newfoundland. Through these waters there pass many ships of many flags. They bear food and other supplies to civilians; and they bear materiel of war, for which the people of the United States are spending billions of dollars, and which, by Congressional action, they have declared to be essential for the defense of our own land.

The United States destroyer, when attacked, was proceeding on a legitimate mission.

If the destroyer was visible to the submarine when the torpedo was fired, then the attack was a deliberate attempt by the Nazis to sink a clearly identified American warship.

On the other hand, if the submarine was beneath the surface of the sea and, with the aid of its listening devices, fired in the direction of the sound of the American destroyer without even taking the trouble to learn its identity, as the official German communique would indicate, then the attack was even more outrageous. For it indicates a policy of indiscriminate violence against any vessel sailing the seas, belligerent or non-belligerent.

This was piracy, piracy legally and morally. It was not the first nor the last act of piracy which the Nazi government has committed against the American flag in this war, for attack has followed attack.

A few months ago an American-flag merchant ship, the Robin Moor, was sunk by a Nazi submarine in the middle of the South Atlantic, under circumstances violating long-established international law and violating every principle of humanity. The passengers and the crew were forced into open boats hundreds of miles from land, in direct violation of international agreements signed by nearly all nations, including the government of Germany. No apology, no allegation of mistake, no offer of reparations has come from the Nazi government.

In July, 1941, nearly two months ago, an American battleship in North American waters was followed by a submarine which for a long time sought to manoeuver itself into a position of attack upon the battleship. The periscope of the submarine was clearly seen. No British or American submarines were within hundreds of miles of this spot at the time, so the nationality of the submarine was clear.

Five days ago a United States Navy ship on patrol picked up three survivors of an American-owned ship operating under the flag of our sister republic of Panama, the S.S. Sessa.

On Aug. 17 she had been first torpedoed without warning, and then shelled, near Greenland, while carrying civilian supplies to Iceland. It is feared that the other members of her crew have been drowned. In view of the established presence of German submarines in this vicinity, there can be no reasonable doubt as to the identity of the flag of the attacker.

Five days ago another United States merchant ship, the Steel Seafarer, was sunk by a German aircraft in the Red Sea 220 miles south of Suez. She was bound for an Egyptian port.

So four of the vessels sunk or attacked flew the American flag and were clearly identifiable. Two of these ships were warships of the American Navy. In the fifth case the vessel sunk clearly carried the flag of our sister republic of Panama.

In the face of all this we Americans are keeping our feet on the ground. Our type of democratic civilization has outgrown the thought of feeling compelled to fight some other nation by reason of any single piratical attack on one of our ships. We are not becoming hysterical or losing our sense of proportion. Therefore, what I am thinking and saying tonight does not relate to any isolated episode.

Instead, we Americans are taking a long-range point of view in regard to certain fundamentals, a point of view in regard to a series of events on land and on sea which must be considered as a whole, as a part of a world pattern.

It would be unworthy of a great nation to exaggerate an isolated incident, or to become inflamed by some one act of violence. But it would be inexcusabe folly to minimize such incidents in the face of evidence which makes it clear that the incident is not isolated, but part of a general plan.

The important truth is that these acts of international lawlessness are a manifestation of a design, a design that has been made clear to the American people for a long time. It is the Nazi design to abolish the freedom of the seas and to acquire absolute control and domination of these seas for themselves.

For with control of the seas in their own hands, the way can become obviously clear for their next step, domination of the United States, domination of the Western Hemisphere by force of arms. Under Nazi control of the seas no merchant ship of the United States or of any other American republic would be free to carry on any peaceful commerce, except by the condescending grace of this foreign and tyrannical power.

The Atlantic Ocean, which has been and which should always be a free and friendly highway for us, would then become a deadly menace to the commerce of the United States, to the coasts of the United States and even to the inland cities of the United States.

The Hitler government, in defiance of the laws of the sea, in defiance of the recognized rights of all nations, has presumed to declare, on paper, that great areas of the seas, even including a vast expanse lying in the Western Hemisphere, are to be closed and that no ships may enter them for any purpose, except at peril of being sunk. Actually they are sinking ships at will and without warning in widely separated areas both within and far outside of these farflung pretended zones.

This Nazi attempt to seize control of the oceans is but a counterpart of the Nazi plots now being carried on throughout the Western Hemisphere, all designed toward the same end. For Hitler's advance guards, not only his avowed agents but also his dupes among us, have sought to make ready for him footholds and bridgeheads in the New World, to be used as soon as he has gained control of the oceans.

His intrigues, his plots, his machinations, his sabotage in this New World are all known to the Government of the United States. Conspiracy has followed conspiracy.

For example, last year a plot to seize the government of Uruguay was smashed by the prompt action of that country, which was supported in full by her American neighbors. A like plot was then hatching in Argentina, and the government has carefully and wisely blocked it at every point. More recently an endeavor was made to subvert the government of Bolivia and within the past few weeks the discovery was made of secret air landing fields in Colombia within easy range of the Panama Canal. I could multiply instance upon instance.

To be ultimately successful in world mastery, Hitler knows that he must get control of the seas. He must first destroy the bridge of ships which we are building across the Atlantic and over which we shall continue to roll the implements of war to help destroy him, to destroy all his works in the end. He must wipe out our patrol on sea and in the air if he is to do it. He must silence the British Navy.

I think it must be explained over and over again to people who like to think of the United States Navy as an invincible protection that this can be true only if the British Navy survives. And that, my friends, is simple arithmetic.

For if the world outside of the Americas falls under Axis domination, the shipbuilding facilities which the Axis powers would then possess in all of Europe, in the British Isles and in the Far East would be much greater than all the shipbuilding facilities and potentialities of all of the Americas, not only greater, but two or three times greater—enough to win.

Even if the United States threw all its resources into such a situation, seeking to double and even redouble the size of our Navy, the Axis powers, in control of the rest of the world, would have the man power and the physical resources to outbuild us several times over.

It is time for all Americans of all the Americas to stop being deluded by the romantic notion that the Americas can go on living happily and peacefully in a Nazi-dominated world.

Generation after generation, America has battled for the general policy of the freedom of the seas. And that policy is a very simple one—but a basic, a fundamental one. It means that no nation has the right to make the broad oceans of the world at great distances from the actual theatre of land war unsafe for the commerce of others.

That has been our policy, proved time and time again, in all our history.

Our policy has applied from the earliest days of the republic and still applies, not merely to the Atlantic but to the Pacific and to all other oceans as well.

Unrestricted warfare in 1941 continues a defiance—an act of aggression—against that historic American policy.

It is now clear that Hitler has begun his campaign to control the seas by ruthless force and by wiping out every vestige of international law, every vestige of humanity.

His intention has been made clear. The American people can have no further illusions about it.

No tender whisperings of appeasers that Hitler is not interested in the Western Hemisphere, no soporific lullabies that a wide ocean protects us from him can long have any effect on the hardheaded, far-sighted and realistic American people.

Because of these episodes, because of the movements and operations of German warships, and because of the clear, repeated proof that the present government of Germany has no respect for treaties or for international law, that it has no decent attitude toward neutral nations or human life—we Americans are now face to face not with abstract theories but with cruel, relentless facts.

This attack on the Greer was no localized military operation in the North Atlantic. This was no mere episode in a struggle between two nations. This was one determined step toward creating a permanent world system based on force, on terror and on murder.

I am sure that even now the Nazis are waiting, waiting to see whether the United States will by silence give them the green light to go ahead on this path of destruction.

The Nazi danger to our Western World has long ceased to be a mere possibility. The danger is here now—not only from a military enemy but from an enemy of all law, all liberty, all morality, all religion.

There has now come a time when you and I must see the cold inexorable necessity of saying to these inhuman, unrestrained seekers of world conquest and permanent world domination by the sword—"You seek to throw our children and our children's children into your form of terrorism and slavery. You have now attacked our own safety. You shall go no further."

Normal practices of diplomacy—note writing—are of no possible use in dealing with international outlaws who sink our ships and kill our citizens.

One peaceful nation after another has met disaster because each refused to look the Nazi danger squarely in the eye, until it actually had them by the throat.

The United States will not make that fatal mistake.

No act of violence, no act of intimidation will keep us from maintaining intact two bulwarks of defense: First, our line of supply of materiel to the enemies of Hitler, and second, the freedom of our shipping on the high seas.

No matter what it takes, no matter what it costs, we will keep open the line of legitimate commerce in these defensive waters of ours.

We have sought no shooting war with Hitler. We do not seek it now. But neither do we want peace so much that we are willing to pay for it by permitting him to attack our naval and merchant ships while they are on legitimate business.

I assume that the German leaders are not deeply concerned tonight, or any other time, by what the real Americans or the American Government says or publishes about them. We cannot bring about the downfall of Nazism by the use of long-range invective.

But when you see a rattlesnake poised to strike, you do not wait until he has struck before you crush him.

These Nazi submarines and raiders are the rattlesnakes of the Atlantic. They are a menace to the free pathways of the high seas. They are a challenge to our sovereignty. They hammer at our most precious rights when they attack ships of the American flag—symbols of our independence, our freedom, our very life.

It is clear to all Americans that the time has come when the Americas themselves must now be defended. A continuation of attacks in our own waters, or in waters which could be used for further and greater attacks on us, will inevitably weaken American ability to repel Hitlerism.

Do not let us be hair-splitters. Let us not ask ourselves whether the Americas should begin to defend themselves after the first attack, or the fifth attack, or the tenth attack, or the twentieth attack.

The time for active defense is now.

Do not let us split hairs. Let us not say, "We will only defend ourselves if the torpedo succeeds in getting home, or if the crew and the passengers are drowned."

This is the time for prevention of attack.

If submarines or raiders attack in distant waters, they can attack equally within sight of our own shores. Their very presence in any waters which America deems vital to its defense constitutes an attack.

In the waters which we deem necessary for our defense American naval vessels and American planes will no longer wait until Axis submarines lurking under the water, or Axis raiders on the surface of the sea, strike their deadly blow—first.

Upon our naval and air patrol—now operating in large number over a vast expanse of the Atlantic Ocean—falls the duty of maintaining the American policy of freedom of the seas—now. That means, very simply, very clearly, that our patrolling vessels and planes will protect all merchant ships—not only American ships but ship of any flag—engaged in commerce in our defensive waters.

They will protect them from submarines; they will protect them from surface raiders.

The situation is not new. The second President of the United States, John Adams, ordered the United States Navy to clean out European privateers and European ships of war which were infesting the Caribbean and South American waters, destroying American commerce.

The third President of the United States, Thomas Jefferson, ordered the United States Navy to end the attacks being made upon American and other ships by the corsairs of the nations of North Africa.

My obligation as President is historic; it is clear; yes, it is inescapable.

It is no act of war on our part when we decide to protect the seas that are vital to American defense. The aggression is not ours. Ours is solely defense.

But let this warning be clear. From now on, if German or Italian vessels of war enter the waters the protection of which is necessary for American defense, they do so at their own peril.

The orders which I have given as Commander in Chief of the United States Army and Navy are to carry out that policy—at once.

The sole responsibility rests upon Germany. There will be no shooting unless Germany continues to seek it.

That is my obvious duty in this crisis. That is the clear right of this sovereign nation. This is the only step possible, if we would keep tight the wall of defense which we are pledged to maintain around this Western Hemisphere.

I have no illusions about the gravity of this step. I have not taken it hurriedly or lightly. It is the result of months and months of constant thought and anxiety and prayer. In the protection of your nation and mine it cannot be avoided.

The American people have faced other grave crises in their history—with American courage, with American resolution. They will do no less today.

They know the actualities of the attacks upon us. They know the necessities of a bold defense against these attacks. They know that the times call for clear heads and fearless hearts.

And with that inner strength that comes to a free people conscious of their duty, conscious of the righteousness of what they do, they will—with divine help and guidance—stand their ground against this latest assault upon their democracy, their sovereignty and their freedom.

SPEECH ON PEARL HARBOR
December 9, 1941

My fellow-Americans:
The sudden criminal attacks perpetrated by the Japanese in the Pacific provide the climax of a decade of international immorality.

Powerful and resourceful gangsters have banded together to make war upon the whole human race. Their challenge has now been flung at the United States of America. The Japanese have treacherously violated the long-standing peace between us. Many American soldiers and sailors have been killed by enemy action. American ships have been sunk; American airplanes have been destroyed.

The Congress and the people of the United States have accepted that challenge.

Together with other free peoples, we are now fighting to maintain our right to live among our world neighbors in freedom and in common decency, without fear of assault.

I have prepared the full record of our past relations with Japan, and it will be submitted to the Congress. It begins with the viist of Commodore Perry to Japan eighty-eight years ago. It ends with the visit of two Japanese emissaries to the Secretary of State last Sunday, an hour after Japanese forces had loosed their bombs and machine guns against our flag, our forces and our citizens.

I can say with utmost confidence that no Americans today or a thousand years hence need feel anything but pride in our patience and in our efforts through all the years toward achieving a peace in the Pacific which would be fair and honorable to every nation, large or small. And no honest person, today or a thousand years hence, will be able to suppress a sense of indignation and horror at the treachery committed by the military dictators of Japan under the very shadow of the flag of peace borne by their special envoys in our midst.

The course that Japan has followed for the past ten years in Asia has paralleled the course of Hitler and Mussolini in Europe and in Africa. Today, it has become far more than a parallel. It is collaboration, actual collaboration, so well calculated that all the continents of the world, and all the oceans, are now considered by the Axis strategists as one gigantic battlefield.

In 1931, ten years ago, Japan invaded Manchukuo—without warning.

In 1935, Italy invaded Ethiopia—without warning.

In 1938, Hitler occupied Austria—without warning.

In 1939, Hitler invaded Czecho-Slovakia—without warning.

Later in 1939, Hitler invaded Poland—without warning.

In 1940, Hitler invaded Norway, Denmark, the Netherlands, Belgium and Luxemburg—without warning.

In 1940, Italy attacked France and later Greece—without warning.

And in this year, 1941, the Axis Powers attacked Yugoslavia and Greece and they dominated the Balkans—without warning.

In 1941 also, Hitler invaded Russia—without warning.

And now Japan has attacked Malaya and Thailand—and the United States—without warning.

It is all of one pattern.

We are now in this war. We are all in it—all the way. Every single man, woman and child is a partner in the most tremendous undertaking of our American history. We must share together the bad news and the good news, the defeats and the victories—the changing fortunes of war.

So far, the news has been all bad. We have suffered a serious setback in Hawaii. Our forces in the Philippines, which include the brave people of that commonwealth, are taking punishment, but are defending themselves vigorously. The reports from Guam and Wake and Midway Islands are still confused, but we must be prepared for the announcement that all these three outposts have been seized.

The casualty lists of these first few days will undoubtedly be large. I deeply feel the anxiety of all of the families of the men in our armed forces and the relatives of people in cities which have been bombed. I can only give them my solemn promise that they will get news just as quickly as possible.

This government will put its trust in the stamina of the American people and will give the facts to the public just as soon as two conditions have been fulfilled: first, that the information has been definitely and officially confirmed, and, second, that the release of the information at the time it is received will not prove valuable to the enemy directly or indirectly.

Most earnestly I urge my countrymen to reject all rumors. These ugly little hints of complete disaster fly thick and fast in wartime. They have to be examined and appraised.

As an example, I can tell you frankly that until further surveys are made, I have not sufficient information to state the exact damage which has been done to our naval vessels at Pearl Harbor. Admittedly the damage is serious. But no one can say how serious until we know how much of this damage can be repaired and how quickly the necessary repairs can be made.

I cite as another example a statement made on Sunday night that a Japanese carrier had been located and sunk off the Canal Zone. And when you hear statements that are attributed to what they call "an authoritative source," you can be reasonably sure from now on that under these war circumstances the "authoritative source" is not any person in authority.

Many rumors and reports which we now hear originate, of course, with enemy sources. For instance, today the Japanese are claiming that as a result of their one action against Hawaii they have gained naval supremacy in the Pacific. This is an old trick of propaganda which has been used innumerable times by the Nazis. The purposes of such fantastic claims are, of course, to spread fear and confusion among us and to goad us into revealing military information which our enemies are desperately anxious to obtain.

Our government will not be caught in this obvious trap—and neither will the people of the United States.

It must be remembered by each and every one of us that our free and rapid communication these days must be greatly restricted in wartime. It is not possible to receive full, speedy, accurate reports from distant areas of combat. This is particularly true where naval operations are concerned. For in these days of the marvels of radio it is often impossible for the commanders of various units to report their activities by radio, for the very simple reason that this information would become available to the enemy, and would disclose their position and their plan of defense or attack.

Of necessity there will be delays in officially confirming or denying reports of operations, but we will not hide facts from the country if we know the facts and if the enemy will not be aided by their disclosure.

To all newspapers and radio stations—all those who reach the eyes and ears of the American people—I say this: You have a most grave responsibility to the nation now and for the duration of this war.

If you feel that your government is not disclosing enough of the truth, you have every right to say so. But—in the absence of all the facts, as revealed by official sources—you have no right in the ethics of patriotism to deal out unconfirmed reports in such a way as to make people believe that they are gospel truth.

Every citizen, in every walk of life, shares this same responsibility. The lives of our soldiers and sailors—the whole future of this nation—depend upon the manner in which each and every one of us fulfills his obligation to our country.

Now a word about the recent past—and the future. A year and a half has elapsed since the fall of France, when the whole world first realized the mechanized might which the Axis nations had been building for so many years. America has used that year and a half to great advantage. Knowing that the attack might reach us in all too short a time, we immediately began greatly to increase our industrial strength and our capacity to meet the demands of modern warfare.

Precious months were gained by sending vast quantities of our war material to the nations of the world still able to resist Axis aggression. Our policy rested on the fundamental truth that the defense of any country resisting Hitler or Japan was in the long run the defense of our own country. That policy has been justified. It has given us time, invaluable time, to build our American assembly lines of production.

Assembly lines are now in operation. Others are being rushed to completion. A steady stream of tanks and planes, of guns, ships, and shells and equipment—that is what these eighteen months have given us.

But it is all only a beginning of what still has to be done. We must be set to face a long war against crafty and powerful bandits. The attack at Pearl Harbor can be repeated at any one of many points on both oceans and along both our coast lines and against all the rest of the hemisphere.

It will not only be a long war, it will be a hard war. That is the basis on which we now lay all our plans. That is the yardstick by which we measure what we shall need and demand—money, materials, doubled and quadrupled production—ever increasing. The production must be not only for our own Army and Navy and air forces. It must reinforce the other armies and navies and air forces fighting the Nazis and the war lords of Japan throughout the Americas and throughout the world.

I have been working today on the subject of production. Your government has decided on two broad policies.

The first is to speed up all existing production by working on a seven-day-week basis in every war industry, including the production of essential raw materials.

The second policy, now being put into form, is to rush additions to the capacity of production by building more new plants, by adding to old plants, and by using the many smaller plants for war needs.

Over the hard road of the past months we have at times met obstacles and difficulties, divisions and disputes, indifference and callousness. That is now all past—and, I am sure, forgotten.

The fact is that the country now has an organization in Washington built around men and women who are recognized experts in their own fields. I think the country knows that the people who are actually responsible in each and every one of these many fields are pulling together with a teamwork that has never before been excelled.

On the road ahead there lies hard work—gruelling work—day and night, every hour and every minute.

I was about to add that ahead there lies sacrifice for all of us. But it is not correct to use that word. The United States does not consider it a sacrifice to do all one can, to give one's best to our nation, when the nation is fighting for its existence and its future life.

It is not a sacrifice for any man, old or young, to be in the Army or the Navy of the United States. Rather is it a privilege.

It is not a sacrifice for the industrialist or the wage-earner, the farmer or the shopkeeper, the trainman or the doctor, to pay more taxes, to buy more bonds, to forego extra profits, to work longer or harder at the task for which he is best fitted. Rather, it is a privilege.

It is not a sacrifice to do without many things to which we are accustomed if the national defense calls for doing without them.

A review this morning leads me to the conclusion that at present we shall not have to curtail the normal use of articles of food. There is enough food today for all of us and enough left over to send to those who are fighting on the same side with us.

But there will be a clear and definite shortage of metals for many kinds of civilian use for the very good reason that in our increased program we shall need for war purposes more than half of that portion of the principal metals which during the past year have gone into articles for civilian use. Yes, we shall have to give up many things entirely.

And I am sure that the people in every part of the nation are prepared in their individual living to win this war. I am sure that they will cheerfully help to pay a large part of its financial cost while it goes on. I am sure they will cheerfully give up those material things that they are asked to give up.

And I am sure that they will retain all those great spiritual things without which we cannot win through.

I repeat that the United States can accept no result save victory, final and complete. Not only must the shame of Japanese treachery be wiped out, but the sources of international brutality, wherever they exist, must be absolutely and finally broken.

In my message to the Congress yesterday I said that we "will make very certain that this form of treachery shall never endanger us again." In order to achieve that certainty, we must begin the great task that is before us by abandoning once and for all the illusion that we can ever again isolate ourselves from the rest of humanity.

In these past few years—and, most violently, in the past few days—we have learned a terrible lesson.

It is our obligation to our dead—it is our sacred obligation to their children and to our children—that we must never forget what we have learned.

And what we have learned is this:

There is no such thing as security for any nation—or any individual—in a world ruled by the principles of gangsterism.

There is no such thing as impregnable defense against powerful aggressors who sneak up in the dark and strike without warning.

We have learned that our ocean-girt hemisphere is not immune from severe attack—that we cannot measure our safety in terms of miles on any map any more.

We may acknowledge that our enemies have performed a brilliant feat of deception, perfectly timed and executed with great skill. It was a thoroughly dishonorable deed, but we must face the fact that modern warfare as conducted in the Nazi manner is a dirty business. We don't like it—we didn't want to get in it—but we are in it and we're going to fight it with everything we've got.

I do not think any American has any doubt of our ability to administer proper punishment to the perpetrators of these crimes.

Your government knows that for weeks Germany has been telling Japan that if Japan did not attack the United States, Japan would not share in dividing the spoils with Germany when peace came. She was promised by Germany that if she came in she would receive the complete and perpetual control of the whole of the Pacific area—and that means not only the Far East, but also all of the islands in the Pacific, and also a stranglehold on the west coast of North and Central and South America.

We know also that Germany and Japan are conducting their military and naval operations in accordance with a joint plan. That plan considers all peoples and nations which are not helping the Axis powers as common enemies of each and every one of the Axis powers.

That is their simple and obvious grand strategy. That is why the American people must realize that it can be matched only with similar grand strategy.

We must realize, for example, that Japanese successes against the United States in the Pacific are helpful to German operations in Libya; that any German success against the Caucasus is inevitably an assistance to Japan in her operations against the Dutch East Indies; that a German attack against Algiers or Morocco opens the way to a German attack against South America and the Canal.

On the other side of the picture, we must learn also to know that guerrilla warfare against the Germans in, let us say, Serbia, or Norway, helps us; that a successful Russian offensive against the Germans helps us; and that British success on land or sea in any part of the world strengthens our hands.

Remember always that Germany and Italy, regardless of any formal declaration of war, consider themselves at war with the United States at this moment just as much as they consider themselves at war with Britain or Russia. And Germany puts all the other Republics of the Americas into the same category of enemies. The people of our sister Republics of this Hemisphere can be honored by that fact.

The true goal we seek is far above and beyond the ugly field of battle. When we resort to force, as now we must, we are determined that this force shall be directed toward ultimate good as well as against immediate evil. We Americans are not destroyers —we are builders.

We are now in the midst of a war, not for conquest, not for vengeance, but for a world in which this nation, and all that this nation represents, will be safe for our children. We expect to eliminate the danger from Japan, but it would serve us ill if we accomplished that and found that the rest of the world was dominated by Hitler and Mussolini.

So, we are going to win the war and we are going to win the peace that follows.

And in the difficult hours of this day—and through dark days that may be yet to come—we will know that the vast majority of the members of the human race are on our side. Many of them are fighting with us. All of them are praying for us. For, in representing our cause, we represent theirs as well—our hope and their hope for liberty under God.

MESSAGE TO CONGRESS ON RELATIONS WITH JAPAN
December 15, 1941

To the Congress of the United States of America:

On Dec. 8, 1941, I presented to the Congress a message in person asking for a declaration of war as an answer to the treacherous attack made by Japan the previous day upon the United States.

For the information of the Congress, and as public record of the facts, I am transmitting this historical summary of the past policy of this country in relation to the Pacific area and of the more immediate events leading up to this Japanese onslaught upon our forces and territory. Attached hereto are the various documents and correspondence implementing this history.

I

A little over a hundred years ago, in 1833, the United States entered into its first Far Eastern treaty, a treaty with Siam. It was a treaty providing for peace and for dependable relationships.

Ten years later Caleb Cushing was sent to negotiate and in 1844 there was concluded our first treaty with China.

In 1853, Commodore Perry knocked on Japan's doors. In the next few years those doors began to open; and Japan, which had kept itself aloof from the world, began to adopt what we call Western civilization. During those early years, the United States used every influence it could exert to protect Japan in her transition stage.

With respect to the entire Pacific area, the United States has consistently urged, as it has for all other parts of the globe, the fundamental importance to world peace of fair and equal treatment among nations. Accordingly whenever there has been a tendency on the part of any other nation to encroach upon the independence and sovereignty of countries of the Far East, the United States has tried to discourage such tendency wherever possible.

There was a period when this American attitude was especially important to Japan. At all times it has been important to China and to other countries of the Far East.

At the end of the nineteenth century, the sovereignty of the Philippine Islands passed from Spain to this country. The United States pledged itself to a policy toward the Philippines designed to equip them to become a free and independent nation. That pledge and that policy we have consistently carried out.

At that time there was going on in China what has been called the "scramble for concessions." There was even talk about a possible partitioning of China. It was then that the principle of the "open door" in China was laid down.

In 1900, the American Government declared that its policy was to "seek a solution which may bring about permanent safety and peace to China * * * protect all rights guaranteed to friendly powers by treaty and international law and safeguard for the world the principle of equal and impartial trade with all parts of the Chinese empire."

Ever since that day, we have consistently and unfailingly advocated the principles of the open door policy throughout the Far East.

In the year 1908 the Government of the United States and the Government of Japan concluded an agreement by an exchange of notes. In that agreement, the two governments jointly declared that they were determined to support "by all pacific means at their disposal the independence and integrity of China and the principle of equal opportunity for commerce and industry of all nations in that empire"; that it was "the wish of the two governments to encourage the free and peaceful development of their commerce on the Pacific Ocean"; and that "the policy of both governments" was "directed to the maintenance of the existing status quo" in that region.

The United States has consistently practiced the principles enunciated in that agreement.

In 1921, following the close of the First World War, nine powers having interests in the Western Pacific met in conference in Washington. China, Japan and the United States were there. One great objective of this conference was the maintenance of peace in the Pacific. This was to be achieved by reduction of armament and by regulation of competition in the Pacific and Far Eastern areas. Several treaties and agreements were concluded at that conference.

One of these was the Nine-Power Treaty. It contained pledges to respect the sovereignty of China and the principle of equal opportunity for the commerce and industry of all nations throughout China.

Another was a treaty between the United States, the British Empire, France, Italy and Japan providing for limitation of naval armament.

The course of events which have led directly to the present crisis began ten years ago. For it was then, in 1931, that Japan undertook on a large scale its present policy of conquest in China. It began by the invasion of Manchuria, which was part of China. The Council and the Assembly of the League of Nations, at once and during many months of continuous effort thereafter, tried to persuade Japan to stop.

The United States supported that effort. For example, the government of the United States on Jan. 7, 1932, specifically stated in notes sent to the Japanese and the Chinese Governments that it would not recognize any situation, treaty or agreement brought about by violation of treaties.

This barbaric aggression of Japan in Manchuria set the example and the pattern for the course soon to be pursued by Italy and Germany in Africa and in Europe. In 1933 Hitler assumed power in Germany. It was evident that, once rearmed, Germany would embark upon a policy of conquest in Europe. Italy—then still under the domination of Mussolini—also had resolved upon a policy of conquest in Africa and in the Mediterranean.

Through the years which followed, Germany, Italy and Japan reached an understanding to time their acts of aggression to their common advantage —and to bring about the ultimate enslavement of the rest of the world.

In 1934 the Japanese Minister for Foreign Affairs sent a friendly note to the United States stating that he firmly believed that no question existed between the two governments that was "fundamentally incapable of amicable solution." He added that Japan had "no intention whatever to provoke and make trouble with any other power." Our Secretary of State, Cordell Hull, replied in kind.

But in spite of this exchange of friendly sentiments, and almost immediately thereafter, the acts and utterances of the Japanese Government began to belie these assurances—at least so far as the rights and interests of other nations in China were concerned.

Our government thereupon expressed to Japan the view of the American people, and of the American Government, that no nation has the right thus to override the rights and legitimate interests of other sovereign states.

The structure of peace which has been founded upon the Washington Conference treaties began to be discarded by Japan. Indeed, in December of 1934, the Japanese Government gave notice of its intention to terminate the Naval Treaty of Feb. 6, 1922, which had limited competition in naval armament. She thereafter intensified and multiplied her rearmament program.

In 1936 the government of Japan openly associated itself with Germany by entering the Anti-Comintern Pact.

This pact, as we all know, was nominally directed against the Soviet Union; but its real purpose was to form a league of fascism against the free world, particularly against Great Britain, France and the United States.

Following the association of Germany, Italy and Japan, the stage was now set for an unlimited campaign of conquest. In July, 1937, feeling themselves ready, the armed forces of Japan opened new large-scale military operations against China. Presently her leaders, dropping the mask of hypocrisy, publicly declared their intention to seize and maintain for Japan a dominant position in the entire region of Eastern Asia, the Western Pacific and the Southern Pacific.

They thus accepted the German thesis that seventy or eighty million Germans were by race, training, ability and might superior in every way to any other race in Europe—superior to about four hundred million other human beings in that area. And Japan, following suit, announced that the seventy or eighty million Japanese people were also superior to the seven or eight hundred million other inhabitants of the Orient—nearly all of whom were infinitely older and more developed in culture and civilization than themselves.

Their conceit would make them masters of a region containing almost one-half the population of the earth. It would give them complete control of vast sea lanes and trade routes of importance to the entire world.

The military operations which followed in China flagrantly disregarded American rights. Japanese armed forces killed Americans. They wounded or abused American men, women and children. They sank American vessels, including a naval vessel, the Panay. They bombed American hospitals, churches, schools and missions. They destroyed American property. They obstructed, and in some cases drove out, American commerce.

In the meantime they were inflicting incalculable damage upon China and ghastly suffering upon the Chinese people. They were inflicting wholesale injuries upon other nations, flouting all the principles of peace and good-will among men.

There are attached hereto lists of American nationals killed or wounded by Japanese forces in China since July 7, 1937; of American property in China reported to have been damaged, destroyed or seriously endangered by Japanese air bombing or air machine-gunning; of American nationals reported to have been assaulted, arbitrarily detained or subjected to indignities; of interference with American nationals' rights and interests.

These lists are not complete. However, they are ample evidence of the flagrant Japanese disregard of American rights and civilized standards.   II

Meanwhile brute conquest was on the rampage in Europe and the Mediterranean.

Hitler and Mussolini embarked upon a scheme of unlimited conquest. Since 1935, without provocation or excuse, they have attacked, conquered and reduced to economic and political slavery some sixteen independent nations. The machinery set up for their unlimited conquest included, and still includes, not only enormous armed forces but also huge organizations for carrying on plots, intrigue, intimidation, propaganda and sabotage. This machine, unprecedented in size, has world-wide ramifications; and into them the Japanese plans and operations have been steadily interlocked.

As the forces of Germany, Italy and Japan increasingly combined their efforts over these years I was convinced that this combination would ultimately attack the United States and the Western Hemisphere, if it were successful in the other continents.

The very existence of the United States as a great free people, and the free existence of the American family of nations in the New World, would be a standing challenge to the Axis. The Axis dictators would choose their own time to make it clear that the United States and the New World were included in their scheme of destruction.

This they did last year, in 1940, when Hitler and Mussolini concluded a treaty of alliance with Japan deliberately aimed at the United States.

The strategy of Japan in the Pacific area was a faithful counterpart of that used by Hitler in Europe. Through infiltration, encirclement, intimidation, and finally armed attack, control was extended over neighboring peoples. Each such acquisition was a new starting point for new aggression.

III

Pursuing this policy of conquest, Japan had first worked her way into and finally seized Manchuria. Next she had invaded China, and has sought for the past four and one-half years to subjugate her. Passing through the China Sea close to the Philippine Islands, she then invaded and took possession of Indo-China. Today the Japanese are extending this conquest throughout Thailand and seeking the occupation of Malaya and Burma. The Philippines, Borneo, Sumatra, Java, come next on the Japanese timetable; and it is probable that further down the Japanese page are the names of Australia, New Zealand and all the other islands of the Pacific, including Hawaii and the great chain of the Aleutian Islands.

To the eastward of the Philippines Japan violated the mandate under which she had received the custody of the Caroline, Marshall and Mariana Islands after the World War by fortifying them, and not only closing them to all commerce but her own, but forbidding any foreigner even to visit them.

Japanese spokesmen, after their custom, cloaked these conquests with innocent-sounding names. They talked of the "new order in

Eastern Asia," and then of the "co-prosperity sphere in Greater East Asia." What they really intended was the enslavement of every nation which they could bring within their power and the enrichment—not of all Asia, not even of the common people of Japan—but of the war lords who had seized control of the Japanese state. Here, too, they were following the Nazis' pattern.

By this course of aggression Japan made it necessary for various countries, including our own, to keep in the Pacific in self-defense large armed forces and a vast amount of material which might otherwise have been used against Hitler. That, of course, is exactly what Hitler wanted them to do. The diversion thus created by Hitler's Japanese ally forced the peace-loving nations to establish and maintain a huge front in the Pacific.

IV

Throughout this course and program of Japanese aggression, the Government of the United States consistently endeavored to persuade the Government of Japan that Japan's best interests would lie in maintaining and cultivating friendly relations with the United States and with all other countries that believe in orderly and peaceful processes.

Following the outbreak of hostilities between Japan and China in 1937, this government made known to the Japanese Government and to the Chinese Government that whenever both those governments considered it desirable we stood ready to exercise our good offices. During the following years of conflict that attitude on our part remained unchanged.

In October, 1937, upon invitation by which the Belgian Government made itself the host, nineteen countries which have interests in the Far East, including the United States, sent representatives to Brussels to consider the situation in the Far East in conformity with the Nine Power Treaty and to endeavor to bring about an adjustment of the difficulties between Japan and China by peaceful means.

Japan and Germany only of all the powers invited declined to attend. Japan was itself an original signatory of the treaty. China, one of the signatories, and the Soviet Union, not a signatory, attended. After the conference opened, the countries in attendance made further attempts to persuade Japan to participate in the conference. Japan again declined.

On Nov. 24, 1937, the conference adopted a declaration, urging that "hostilities be suspended and resort be had to peaceful processes." Japan scorned the conference and ignored the recommendation.

It became clear that, unless this course of affairs in the Far East was halted, the Pacific area was doomed to experience the same horrors which have devastated Europe.

Therefore, in this year of 1941, in an endeavor to end this process by peaceful means while there seemed still to be a chance, the United States entered into discussion with Japan. For nine months these conversations were carried on for the purpose of arriving at some understanding acceptable to both countries.

Throughout all of these conversations this government took into account not only the legitimate interests of the United States but also those of Japan and other countries. When questions relating to the legitimate rights and interests of other countries came up this government kept in appropriate contact with the representatives of those countries.

In the course of these negotiations, the United States steadfastly advocated certain basic principles which should govern international relations. These were:

The principle of inviolability of territorial integrity and sovereignty of all nations.

The principle of noninterference in the internal affairs of other countries.

The principle of equality, including equality of commercial opportunity and treatment.

The principle of reliance upon international cooperation and conciliation for the prevention, and pacific settlement, of controversies.

The Japanese Government, it is true, repeatedly offered qualified statements of peaceful intention. But it became clear, as each proposal was explored, that Japan did not intend to modify in any way her greedy designs upon the whole Pacific world. Although she continually maintained that she was promoting only the peace and greater prosperity of East Asia, she continued her brutal assault upon the Chinese people.

Nor did Japan show an inclination to renounce her unholy alliance with Hitlerism.

In July of this year the Japanese Government connived with Hitler to force from the Vichy Government of France permission to place Japanese armed forces in Southern Indo-China; and began sending her troops and equipment into that area.

The conversations between this government and the Japanese Government were thereupon suspended. But during the following month, at the urgent and insistent request of the Japanese Government, which again made emphatic profession of peaceful intent, the conversations were resumed.

At that time the Japanese Government made the suggestion that the responsible heads of the Japanese Government and of the government of the United States meet personally to discuss means for bringing about an adjustment of relations between the two countries.

I should have been happy to travel thousands of miles to meet the Premier of Japan for that purpose. But I felt it desirable, before so doing, to obtain some assurance that there could be some agreement on basic principles. This government tried hard, but without success, to obtain such assurance from the Japanese Government.

The various proposals of the Japanese Government and the attitude taken by this government are set forth in a document which the Secretary of State handed to the Japanese Ambassador on Oct. 2, 1941.

Thereafter, several formula were offered and discussed. But the Japanese Government continued upon its course of war and conquest.

Finally, on Nov. 20, 1941, the Japanese Government presented a new and narrow proposal which called for supplying by the United States to Japan of as much oil as Japan might require, for suspension of freezing measures, and for discontinuance by the United States to aid China. It contained, however, no provision for abandonment by Japan of her warlike operations or aims.

Such a proposal obviously offered no basis for a peaceful settlement or even for a temporary adjustment. The American Government, in order to clarify the issues, presented to the Japanese Government on Nov. 26 a clear-cut plan for a broad but simple settlement.

The outline of the proposed plan for agreement between the United States and Japan was divided into two parts:

In Section I there was outlined a mutual declaration of policy containing affirmations that the national policies of the two countries were directed toward peace throughout the Pacific area, that the two countries had no territorial designs or aggressive intentions in that area, and that they would give active support to certain fundamental principles of peace upon which their relations with each other and all other nations would be based.

There was provision for mutual pledges to support and apply in their economic relations with each other and with other nations and peoples liberal economic principles, which were enumerated, based upon the general principle of equality of commercial opportunity and treatment.

In Section II there were outlined proposed steps to be taken by the two governments. These steps envisaged a situation in which there would be no Japanese or other foreign armed forces in French Indo-China or in China. Mutual commitments were suggested along lines as follows:

(a) To endeavor to conclude a multilateral non-aggression pact among the governments principally concerned in the Pacific area;

(b) To endeavor to conclude among the principally interested governments an agreement to respect the territorial integrity of

Indo-China and not to seek or accept preferential economic treatment therein;

(c) Not to support any government in China other than the National Government of the Republic of China, with capital temporarily at Chungking;

(d) To relinquish extraterritorial and related rights in China and to endeavor to obtain the agreement of other governments now possessing such rights to give up those rights;

(e) To negotiate a trade agreement based upon reciprocal most-favored-nation treatment;

(f) To remove freezing restrictions imposed by each country on the funds of the other;

(g) To agree upon a plan for the stabilization of the dollar-yen rate;

(h) To agree that no agreement which either had concluded with any third power or powers shall be interpreted by it in a way to conflict with the fundamental purpose of this agreement; and

(i) To use their influence to cause other governments to adhere to the basic political and economic principles provided for in this suggested agreement.

In the midst of these conversations we learned that new contingents of Japanese armed forces and new masses of equipment were moving into Indo-China. Toward the end of November these movements were intensified. During the first week of December new movements of Japanese forces made it clear that, under cover of the negotiations, attacks on unspecified objectives were being prepared.

I promptly asked the Japanese Government for a frank statement of the reasons for increasing its forces in Indo-China. I was given an evasive and specious reply. Simultaneously, the Japanese operations went forward with increased tempo.

We did not know then, as we know now, that they had ordered and were even then carrying out their plan for a treacherous attack upon us.

I was determined, however, to exhaust every conceivable effort for peace. With this in mind, on the evening of Dec. 6 last I addressed a personal message to the Emperor of Japan.

To this government's proposal of Nov. 26 the Japanese Government made no reply until Dec. 7. On that day the Japanese Ambassador here and the special representative whom the Japanese Government had sent to the United States to assist in peaceful negotiations delivered a lengthy document to our Secretary of State one hour after the Japanese had launched a vicious attack upon American territory and American citizens in the Pacific.

That document was a few minutes after its receipt aptly characterized by the Secretary of State as follows:

"I must say that in all my conversations with you (the Japanese Ambassador) during the last nine months I have never uttered one word of untruth. This is borne out absolutely by the record. In all my fifty years of public service I have never seen a document that was more crowded with infamous falsehoods and distortions— infamous falsehoods and distortions on a scale so huge that I never imagined until today that any government on this planet was capable of uttering them."

I concur emphatically in every word of the statement.

For the record of history, it is essential in reading this part of my message always to bear in mind that the actual air and submarine attack in the Hawaiian Islands commenced on Sunday, Dec. 7, at 1:20 P.M., Washington time—7:50 A.M. Honolulu time of same day—Monday, Dec. 8, 3:20 A.M., Tokyo time.

To my message of Dec. 6 (9 P.M. Washington time—Dec. 7, 11 A.M. Tokyo time) to the Emperor of Japan, invoking his cooperation with me in further effort to preserve peace, there has finally come to me on Dec. 10 (6:23 A.M. Washington time—Dec. 10, 8:23 P.M. Tokyo time) a reply, conveyed in a telegraphic report by the American Ambassador at Tokyo dated Dec. 8, 1 P.M. (Dec. 7, 11 P.M. Washington time).

The Ambassador reported at 7 o'clock on the morning of the 8th (Dec. 7, 5 P.M. Washington time) the Japanese Minister of Foreign Affairs asked him to call at his official residence; that the Foreign Minister handed the Ambassador a memorandum dated Dec. 8 (Dec. 7 Washington time) the text of which had been transmitted to the Japanese Ambassador in Washington to be presented to the American Government (this was the memorandum which was delivered by the Japanese Ambassador to the Secretary of State at 2:20 P.M. on Sunday, Dec. 7 (Monday, Dec. 8, 4:20 A.M. Tokyo time); that the Foreign Minister had been in touch with the Emperor; and that the Emperor desired that the memorandum be regarded as the Emperor's reply to my message.

Further, the Ambassador reports, the Foreign Minister made an oral statement. Textually, the oral statement began "His Majesty has expressed his gratefulness and appreciation for the cordial message of the President."

The message further continued to the effect that, in regard to our inquiries on the subject of increase of Japanese forces in French Indo-China, His Majesty had commanded his government to state its views to the American Government. The message continued, textually, with the statement:

"Establishment of peace in the Pacific, and consequently of the world, has been the cherished desire of His Majesty for the realization of which he has hitherto made his government to continue its earnest endeavors. His Majesty trusts that the President is fully aware of this fact."

Japan's real reply, however, made by Japan's war lords and evidently formulated many days before, took the form of the attack which had already been made without warning upon our territories at various points in the Pacific.

There is the record, for all history to read in amazement, in sorrow, in horror and in disgust.

We are now at war. We are fighting in self-defense. We are fighting in defense of our national existence, of our right to be secure, of our right to enjoy the blessings of peace. We are fighting in defense of principles of law and order and justice, against an effort of unprecedented ferocity to overthrow those principles and to impose upon humanity a regime of ruthless domination by unrestricted and arbitrary force.

Other countries, too—a host of them—have declared war on Japan. Some of them were first attacked by Japan, as we have been. China has already been valiantly resisting Japan in an undeclared war forced upon her by Japan. After four and one-half years of stubborn resistance, the Chinese now and henceforth will fight with renewed confidence and confirmed assurance of victory.

All members of the great British Commonwealth, themselves fighting heroically on many fronts against Germany and her allies, have joined with us in the Battle of the Pacific, as we have joined with them in the Battle of the Atlantic.

All but three of the governments of nations overrun by German armies have declared war on Japan. The other three are severing relations.

In our own hemisphere many of our sister republics have declared war on Japan, and the others have given firm expression of their solidarity with the United States.

The following are the countries which have to date declared war against Japan:

Australia, Canada, China, Costa Rica, Cuba, Dominican Republic, Guatemala, Haiti, Honduras, The Netherlands, Nicaragua, New Zealand, Panama, El Salvador, South Africa, United Kingdom, Poland.

These and other peace-loving countries will be fighting as we are, first, to put an end to Japan's program of aggression, and, second, to make good the right of nations and of mankind to live in peace under conditions of security and justice.

The people of this country are totally united in their determination to consecrate our national strength and man power to bring conclusively to an end the pestilence of aggression and force which has long menaced the world and which now has struck deliberately and directly at the safety of the United States.

MESSAGE TO CONGRESS

on January 6, 1942

In fulfilling my duty to report upon the state of the Union, I am proud to say to you that the spirit of the American people was never higher than it is today—the Union was never more closely knit together—this country was never more deeply determined to face the solemn tasks before it.

The response of the American people has been instantaneous. It will be sustained until our security is assured.

Exactly one year ago today I said to this Congress: "When the dictators are ready to make war upon us, they will not wait for an act of war on our part . . . They—not we—will choose the time and the place and the method of their attack."

We now know their choice of the time: a peaceful Sunday morning—December 7, 1941.

We know their choice of the place: an American outpost in the Pacific.

We know their choice of the method: the method of Hitler himself.

Japan's scheme of conquest goes back half a century. It was not merely a policy of seeking living room: it was a plan which included the subjugation of all the peoples in the Far East and in the islands of the Pacific, and the domination of that ocean by Japanese military and naval control of the western coasts of North Central and South America.

The development of this ambitious conspiracy was marked by the war against China in 1894; the subsequent occupation of Korea; the war against Russia in 1904; the illegal fortification of the mandated Pacific islands following 1920; the seizure of Manchuria in 1931; and the invasion of China in 1937.

A similar policy of criminal conquest was adopted by Italy. The Fascists first revealed their imperial designs in Libya and Tripoli.

in 1935 they seized Abyssinia. Their goal was the domination of all North Africa, Egypt, parts of France, and the entire Mediterranean world.

But the dreams of empire of the Japanese and Fascist leaders were modest in comparison with the Gargantuan aspirations of Hitler and his Nazis. Even before they came to power in 1933, their plans for conquest had been drawn. Those plans provided for ultimate domination, not of any one section of the world but of the whole earth and all the oceans on it.

With Hitler's formation of the Berlin-Rome-Tokyo alliance, all of these plans of conquest became a single plan. Under this, in addition to her own schemes of conquest, Japan's role was to cut off our supply of weapons of war to Britain, Russia, and China— weapons which increasingly were speeding the day of Hitler's doom. The act of Japan at Pearl Harbor was intended to stun us—to terrify us to such an extent that we would divert our industrial and military strength to the Pacific area or even to our own continental defense.

The plan failed in its purpose. We have not been stunned. We have not been terrified or confused. This reassembling of the Seventy-seventh Congress is proof of that; for the mood of quiet, grim resolution which here prevails bodes ill for those who conspired and collaborated to murder world peace.

That mood is stronger than any mere desire for revenge. It expresses the will of the American people to make very certain that the world will never so suffer again.

Admittedly, we have been faced with hard choices. It was bitter, for example, not to be able to relieve the heroic defenders of Wake Island. It was bitter for us not to be able to land a million men and a thousand ships in the Philippine Islands.

But this adds only to our determination to see to it that the Stars and Stripes will fly again over Wake and Guam; and that the brave people of the Philippines will be rid of Japanese imperialism, and will live in freedom, security, and independence.

Powerful and offensive actions must and will be taken in proper time. The consolidations of the United Nations' total war effort against our common enemies is being achieved.

That is the purpose of conferences which have been held during the past two weeks in Washington, in Moscow, and in Chungking. That is the primary objective of the declaration of solidarity signed in Washington on January 1st, 1942, by 26 nations united against the Axis powers.

Difficult choices may have to be made in the months to come. We will not shrink from such decisions. We and those united with us will make those decisions with courage and determination.

Plans have been laid here and in the other capitals for coordinated and cooperative action by all the United Nations—military action and economic action. Already we have established unified command of land, sea, and air forces in the southwestern Pacific theater of war. There will be a continuation of conferences and consultations among military staffs, so that the plans and operations of each will fit into a general strategy designed to crush the enemy. We shall not fight isolated wars—each nation going its own way. These 26 nations are united—not in spirit and determination alone but in the broad conduct of the war in all its phases.

For the first time since the Japanese and the Fascists and the Nazis started along their blood-stained course of conquest they now face the fact that superior forces are assembling against them. Gone forever are the days when the aggressors could attack and destroy their victims one by one without unity of resistance. We of the United Nations will so dispose of our forces that we can strike at the common enemy wherever the greatest damage can be done.

The militarists in Berlin and Tokyo started this war. But the massed, angered forces of common humanity will finish it.

Destruction of the material and spiritual centers of civilization —this has been and still is the purpose of Hitler and his Italian and Japanese chessmen. They would wreck the power of the British Commonwealth and Russia and China and the Netherlands—and then combine all their forces to achieve their ultimate goal, the conquest of the United States.

They know that victory for us means victory for freedom.

They know that victory for us means victory for the institution of democracy—the ideal of the family, the simple principles of common decency and humanity.

They know that victory for us means victory for religion.

And they could not tolerate that. The world is too small to provide adequate "living room" for both Hitler and God. In proof of that, the Nazis have now announced their plan for enforcing their new German, pagan religion throughout the world—the plan by which the Holy Bible and the Cross of Mercy would be displaced by MEIN KAMPF and the swastika and the naked sword.

Our own objectives are clear: the objective of smashing the militarism imposed by the warlords upon their enslaved peoples—the objective of liberating the subjugated nations—the objective of establishing and securing freedom of speech, freedom of religion, freedom from want, and freedom from fear everywhere in the world.

We shall not stop short of these objectives—nor shall we be satisfied merely to gain them and then call it a day. I know that I speak for the American people—and I have good reason to believe I speak also for all the other peoples who fight with us—when I say that this time we are determined not only to win the war but also to maintain the security of the peace which will follow.

But modern methods of warfare make it a task not only of shooting and fighting, but an even more urgent one of working and producing.

Victory requires the actual weapons of war and the means of transporting them to a dozen points of combat.

It will not be sufficient for us and the other United Nations to produce a slightly superior supply of munitions to that of Germany, Japan, Italy, and the stolen industries in the countries which they have overrun.

The superiority of the United Nations in munitions and ships must be overwhelming—so overwhelming that the Axis nations can never hope to catch up with it. In order to attain this overwhelming superiority the United Nations must build planes and tanks and guns and ships to the utmost limit of our national capacity. We have the ability and capacity to produce arms not only for our own forces but also for the armies, navies, and air forces fighting on our side.

And our overwhelming superiority of armament must be adequate to put weapons of war at the proper time into the hands of those men in the conquered nations, who stand ready to seize the first opportunity to revolt against their German and Japanese aggressors, and against the traitors in their own ranks, known by the already infamous name of "Quislings." As we get guns to the patriots in those lands, they too will fire shots heard 'round the world.

This production of ours in the United States must be raised far above its present levels, even though it will mean the dislocation of the lives and occupations of millions of our own people. We must raise our sights all along the production-line. Let no man say it cannot be done. It must be done—and we have undertaken to do it.

I have just sent a letter of directive to the appropriate departments and agencies of our Government, ordering that immediate steps be taken:

1. To increase our production rate of airplanes so rapidly that in this year, 1942, we shall produce 60,000 planes, 10,000 more than the goal set a year and a half ago. This includes 45,000 combat planes—bombers, dive bombers, pursuit planes. The rate of increase will be continued, so that next year, 1943, we shall produce 125,000 planes, including 100,000 combat planes.

2. To increase our production rate of tanks so rapidly that in this year, 1942, we shall produce 45,000 tanks; and to continue that increase so that next year, 1943, we shall produce 75,000 tanks.

3. To increase our production rate of anti-aircraft guns so rapidly that in this year, 1942, we shall produce 20,000 of them; and to continue that increase, so that next year, 1943, we shall produce 35,000 anti-aircraft guns.

4. To increase our production rate of merchant ships so rapidly that in this year, 1942, we shall build 8,000,000 deadweight tons as compared with a 1941 production of 1,100,000. We shall continue that increase so that next year, 1943, we shall build 10,000,000 tons.

These figures and similar figures for a multitude of other implements of war will give the Japanese and Nazis a little idea of just what they accomplished in the attack on Pearl Harbor.

Our task is hard—our task is unprecedented—and the time is short. We must strain every existing armament-producing facility to the utmost. We must convert every available plant and tool to war production. That goes all the way from the greatest plants to the smallest—from the huge automobile industry to the village machine shop.

Production for war is based on men and women—the human hands and brains which collectively we call labor. Our workers stand ready to work long hours; to turn out more in a day's work; to keep the wheels turning and the fires burning 24 hours a day and 7 days a week. They realize well that on the speed and efficiency of their work depend the lives of their sons and their brothers on the fighting fronts.

Production for war is based on metals and raw materials—steel, copper, rubber, aluminum, zinc, tin. Greater and greater quantities of them will have to be diverted to war purposes. Civilian use of them will have to be cut further and still further—and, in many cases, completely eliminated.

War costs money. So far, we have hardly even begun to pay for it. We have devoted only 15 per cent of our national income to our national defense. As will appear in my budget message tomorrow, our war program for the coming fiscal year will cost 56 billion dollars, or, in other words, more than one-half of the estimated annual national income. This means taxes and bonds, and bonds and taxes. It means cutting luxuries and other non-essentials. In a word, it means an "all-out" war by individual effort and family effort in a united country.

Only this all-out scale of production will hasten the ultimate all-out victory. Speed will count. Lost ground can always be regained—lost time never. Speed will save lives; speed will save this Nation which is in peril; speed will save our freedom and civilization—and slowness has never been an Amercan characteristic.

As the United States goes into its full stride, we must always be on guard against misconceptions which will arise naturally or which will be planted among us by our enemies.

We must guard against complacency. We must not underrate the enemy. He is powerful and cunning—and cruel and ruthless. He will stop at nothing which gives him a chance to kill and to destroy. He has trained his people to believe that their highest perfection is achieved by waging war. For many years he has prepared for this very conflict—planning, plotting, training, arming, fighting. We have already tasted defeat. We may suffer further setbacks. We must face the fact of a hard war, a long war, a bloody war, a costly war.

We must, on the other hand, guard against defeatism. That has been one of the chief weapons of Hitler's propaganda machine—used time and again with deadly results. It will not be used successfully on the American people.

We must guard against divisions among ourselves and among all the other United Nations. We must be particularly vigilant against racial discrimination in any of its ugly forms. Hitler will try again to breed mistrust and suspicion between one individual and another, one group and another, one race and another, one government and another. He will try to use the same technique of falsehood and rumor-mongering with which he divided France from Britain. He is trying to do this with us even now. But he will find a unity of will and purpose against him, which will persevere until the destruction of all his black designs upon the freedom and safety of the people of the world.

We cannot wage this war in a defensive spirit. As our power and our resources are fully mobilized, we shall carry the attack against the enemy—we shall hit him and hit him again wherever and whenever we can reach him.

We must keep him far from our shores, for we intend to bring this battle to him on his own home grounds.

American armed forces must be used at any place in all the world where it seems advisable to engage the forces of the enemy. In some cases these operations will be defensive, in order to protect key positions. In other cases, these operations will be offensive, in order to strike at the common enemy, with a view to his complete encirclement and eventual total defeat.

American armed forces will operate at many points in the Far East.

American armed forces will be on all the oceans—helping to guard the essential communications which are vital to the United Nations.

American land and air and sea forces will take stations in the British Isles—which constitute an essential fortress in this world struggle.

American armed forces will help to protect this hemisphere—and also bases outside this hemisphere which could be used for an attack on the Americas.

If any of our enemies from Europe or from Asia attempt long-range raids by "Suicide" squadrons of bombing planes, they will do so only in the hope of terrorizing our people and disrupting our morale. Our people are not afraid of that. We know that we may have to pay a heavy price for freedom. We will pay this price with a will. Whatever the price, it is a thousand times worth it. No matter what our enemies in their desperation may attempt to do to us—we will say, as the people of London have said, "We can take it." And what's more, we can give it back—and we will give it back—with compound interest.

When our enemies challenged our country to stand up and fight, they challenged each and every one of us. And each and every one of us has accepted the challenge—for himself and for the Nation.

There were only some 400 United States Marines who in the heroic and historic defense of Wake Island inflicted such great losses on the enemy. Some of those men were killed in action; and others are now prisoners of war. When the survivors of that great fight are liberated and restored to their homes, they will learn that one hundred and thirty million of their fellow citizens have been inspired to render their own full share of service and sacrifice.

Our men on the fighting fronts have already proved that Americans today are just as rugged and just as tough as any of the heroes whose exploits we celebrate on the Fourth of July.

Many people ask, "When will this war end?" There is only one answer to that. It will end just as soon as we make it end, by our combined efforts, our combined strength, our combined determination to fight through and work through until the end—the end of militarism in Germany and Italy and Japan. Most certainly we shall not settle for less.

That is the spirit in which discussions have been conducted during the visit of the British Prime Minister to Washington. Mr. Churchill and I understand each other, our motives and our purposes. Together, during the past two weeks, we have faced squarely the major military and economic problems of this greatest world war.

All in our Nation have been cheered by Mr. Churchill's visit. We have been deeply stirred by his great message to us. We wish him a safe return to his home. He is welcome in our midst, now and in days to come.

We are fighting on the same side with the British people, who fought alone for long, terrible months and withstood the enemy with fortitude and tenacity and skill.

We are fighting on the same side with the Russian people who have seen the Nazi hordes swarm up to the very gates of Moscow and who, with almost superhuman will and courage, have forced the invaders back into retreat.

We are fighting on the same side as the brave people of China who for four and a half long years have withstood bombs and starvation and have whipped the invaders time and again in spite of superior Japanese equipment and arms.

We are fighting on the same side as the indomitable Dutch.

We are fighting on the same side as all the other governments in exile, whom Hitler and all his armies and all his Gestapo have not been able to conquer.

But we of the United Nations are not making all of this sacrifice of human effort and human lives to return to the kind of world we had after the last world war.

We are fighting today for security, for progress, and for peace, not only for ourselves but for all men, not only for one generation but for all generations. We are fighting to cleanse the world of ancient evils, ancient ills.

Our enemies are guided by brutal cynicism, by unholy contempt for the human race. We are inspired by a faith which goes back all the years to the first chapter of the Book of Genesis: "God created man in His own image."

We on our side are striving to be true to that divine heritage. We are fighting, as our fathers have fought, to uphold the doctrine that all men are equal in the sight of God. Those on the other side are fighting to destroy this deep belief and to create a world in their own image—a world of tyranny and cruelty and serfdom.

That is the conflict that day and night now pervades our lives. No compromise can end that conflict. There never has been—there never can be—successful compromise between good and avil. Only total victory can reward the champions of tolerance and decency and freedom and faith.

ADDRESS ON 60TH BIRTHDAY

January 30, 1942

To all of you who are making tonight's celebrations such a success, I want to say—very simply—thank you.

In the midst of world tragedy—in the midst of sorrow, suffering, destruction and death—it is natural for most of us to say even on a birthday or a feast day: "Isn't the word 'happy' a bit out of place just now?"

That was perhaps my own predominant thought this morning. Yet the day itself and the evening have brought with them a great reassurance which comes from the deep knowledge that most of this world is still ruled by the spirit of Faith, and Hope, and Charity.

Even in time of war those nations, which still hold to the old ideals of Christianity and democracy, are carrying on services to humanity which have little or no relationship to torpedoes or guns or bombs. That means very definitely that we have an abiding faith in the future—a definite expectancy that we are going to win through to a peace which will bring with it continuing progress and substantial success in our efforts for the security and not for the destruction of humanity.

Our enemies must at this moment be wondering—if they are permitted to know what goes on—how we are finding the time during the grim business of war to work for the cause of little children. For, under the enemies' kind of goverment, there is no time for or interest in such things—no time for ideals; no time for decency; no interest in the weak and the afflicted to whom we in this country have dedicated this day.

It would not be strictly true to say that our enemies pay no attention to health or the relief of need. But the difference is this: with them it all comes from the top. It is done only on order from the Ruler. It is carried out by uniformed servants of the Ruler. It is based, in great part, on direction, compulsion and fear. And the

Rulers are concerned not with human beings as human beings but as mere slaves of the state—or cannon fodder.

The United Nations of the world continue, however, to put these things on a very different basis. We support our tasks of humanity in time of war, as in time of peace, through the same old system of telling the public of the great need, and asking for the voluntary help of men, women and children to fill it.

The fight against the disease of infantile paralysis has proven beyond doubt that the way democracy works—the voluntary way—is efficient and successful. It is only ten years ago that this country undertook, through wholly private contributions, to organize every locality to carry on this great effort, not for a year or two, but for all the future years—so long as the fight can help humanity.

Today, as in these many years past, we continue this great crusade—made possible not by a few large gifts but by the dimes and the dollars of the people themselves.

This year there is only one difference proposed for the use of these gifts. The Trustees of the National Foundation for Infantile Paralysis have told me that I can make the special announcement that the authorized County Chapters throughout the Union may use such portion of their share of this year's funds as is necessary to give special assistance to the children of any of our soldiers and sailors and marines who fall victim to infantile paralysis. That will be good news and a well-deserved boon to the fathers who are serving their Flag on land and on sea in many parts of the world, and to the mothers who have been left at home to do their brave part—to carry on.

I am made additionally happy by the fact that in many of our Sister Republics of the Americas, parties and celebrations are being held today to provide needed help to the children in those lands.

For all these reasons I am very sure that this day has not been wasted—that it has been a useful day. For all that you have done, I am very grateful.

For we have all been helpful in lifting some of the clouds of unhappiness and anxiety which have settled down on many of our citizens. In that realization I am sure we shall have added strength to face the days of trial which lie ahead until peace with victory is assured.

The lives of all of us are now dedicated to working and fighting, and, if need be, dying for the cause of a better future—the future that belongs to our little children.

BROADCAST ON WASHINGTON'S BIRTHDAY
February 22, 1942

Washington's Birthday is a most appropriate occasion for us to talk with each other about things as they are today and things as we know they shall be in the future.

For eight years, General Washington and his Continental Army were faced continually with formidable odds and recurring defeats. Supplies and equipment were lacking. In a sense, every winter was a Valley Forge. Throughout the thirteen states there existed fifth columnists—selfish men, jealous men, fearful men, who proclaimed that Washington's cause was hopeless, that he should ask for a negotiated peace.

Washington's conduct in those hard times has provided the model for all Americans ever since—a model of moral stamina. He held to his course, as it had been charted in the Declaration of Independence. He and the brave men who served with him knew that no man's life or fortune was secure, without freedom and free institutions.

The present great struggle has taught us increasingly that freedom of person and security of property anywhere in the world depend upon the security of the rights and obligations of liberty and justice everywhere in the world.

This war is a new kind of war. It is different from all other wars of the past, not only in its methods and weapons but also in its geography. It is warfare in terms of every continent, every island, every sea, every air-lane in the world.

That is the reason why I have asked you to take out and spread before you the map of the whole earth, and to follow with me the references which I shall make to the world-encircling battle lines of this war. Many questions will, I fear, remain unanswered; but I know you will realize I cannot cover everything in any one report to the people.

The broad oceans which have been heralded in the past as our protection from attack have become endless battlefields on which we are constantly being challenged by our enemies.

We must all understand and face the hard fact that our job now is to fight at distances which extend all the way around the globe.

We fight at these vast distances because that is where our enemies are. Until our flow of supplies gives us clear superiority we must keep on striking our enemies wherever and whenever we can meet them, even if, for a while, we have to yield ground. Actually we are taking a heavy toll of the enemy every day that goes by.

We must fight at these vast distances to protect our supply lines and our lines of communication with our allies—protect these lines from the enemies who are bending every ounce of their strength, striving against time, to cut them. The object of the Nazis and the Japanese is to separate the United States, Britain, China and Russia, and to isolate them one from another, so that each will be surrounded and cut off from sources of supplies and reinforcements. It is the old familiar Axis policy of "divide and conquer."

There are those who still think in terms of the days of sailing-ships. They advise us to pull our war ships and our planes and our merchant ships into our home waters and concentrate solely on last ditch defense. But let me illustrate what would happen if we followed such foolish advice.

Look at your map. Look at the vast area of China, with its millions of fighting men. Look at the vast area of Russia, with its powerful armies and proven military might. Look at the British Isles, Australia, New Zealand, the Dutch Indies, India, the Near East and the Continent of Africa, with their resources of raw materials and of peoples determined to resist Axis domination. Look at North America, Central America and South America.

It is obvious what would happen if all these great reservoirs of power were cut off from each other either by enemy action or by self-imposed isolation:

1. We could no longer send aid of any kind to China—to the brave people who, for nearly five years, have withstood Japanese assault, destroyed hundreds of thousands of Japanese soldiers, and vast quantities of Japanese war munitions. It is essential that we help China in her magnificent defense and in her inevitable counter-offensive—for that is one important element in the ultimate defeat of Japan.

2. If we lost communication with the southwest Pacific, all of that area, including Australia and New Zealand, would fall under Japanese domination. Japan could then release great numbers of ships and men to launch attacks on a large scale against the coasts of the Western Hemisphere, including Alaska. At the same time, she could immediately extend her conquests to India, and through the Indian Ocean, to Africa and the Near East.

3. If we were to stop sending munitions to the British and the Russians in the Mediterranean and Persian Gulf areas, we would help the Nazis to overrun Turkey, Syria, Iraq, Persia, Egypt and the Suez Canal, the whole coast of North Africa and the whole coast of West Africa—putting Germany within easy striking distance of South America.

4. If, by such a fatuous policy, we ceased to protect the North Atlantic supply line to Britain and to Russia, we would help to cripple the splendid counter-offensive by Russia against the Nazis, and we would help to deprive Britain of essential food-supplies and munitions.

Those Americans who believed that we could live under the illusion of isolationism wanted the American eagle to imitate the tactics of the ostrich. Now, many of those same people, afraid that we may be sticking our necks out, want our national bird to be turned into a turtle. But we prefer to retain the eagle as it is—flying high and striking hard.

I know that I speak for the mass of the American people when I say that we reject the turtle policy and will continue increasingly the policy of carrying the war to the enemy in distant lands and distant waters—as far as possible from our own home grounds.

There are four main lines of communication now being traveled by our ships: the North Atlantic, the South Atlantic, the Indian Ocean and the South Pacific. These routes are not oneway streets—for the ships which carry our troops and munitions out-bound bring back essential raw materials which we require for our own use.

The maintenance of these vital lines is a very tough job. It is a job which requires tremendous daring, tremendous resourcefulness, and, above all, tremendous production of planes and tanks and guns and of the ships to carry them. And I speak again for the American people when I say that we can and will do that job.

The defense of the world-wide lines of communication demands relatively safe use by us of the sea and of the air along the various routes; and this, in turn, depends upon control by the United Nations of the strategic bases along these routes.

Control of the air involves the simultaneous use of two types of planes—first, the long-range heavy bomber; and, second, light bombers, dive bombers, torpedo planes, and short-range pursuit planes which are essential to the protection of the bases and of the bombers themselves.

Heavy bombers can fly under their own power from here to the southwest Pacific; but the smaller planes cannot. Therefore, these lighter planes have to be packed in crates and sent on board cargo ships. Look at your map again; and you will see that the route is long—and at many places perilous—either across the South Atlantic around South Africa, or from California to the East Indies direct. A vessel can make a round trip by either route in about four months, or only three round trips in a whole year.

In spite of the length and difficulties of this transportation, I can tell you that we already have a large number of bombers and pursuit planes, manned by American pilots, which are now in daily contact with the enemy in the Southwest Pacific. And thousands of American troops are today in that area engaged in operations not only in the air but on the ground as well.

In this battle area, Japan has had an obvious initial advantage. For she could fly even her short-range planes to the points of attack by using many stepping stones open to her—bases in a multitude of Pacific islands and also bases on the China, Indo-China, Thailand and Malay coasts. Japanese troop transports could go south from Japan and China through the narrow China Sea which can be protected by Japanese planes throughout its whole length.

I ask you to look at your maps again, particularly at that portion of the Pacific Ocean lying west of Hawaii. Before this war even started, the Philippine Islands were already surrounded on three sides by Japanese power. On the west, the Japanese were in possession of the coast of China and the coast of Indo-China which had been yielded to them by the Vichy French. On the North, are the islands of Japan themselves, reaching down almost to northern Luzon. On the east, are the Mandated Islands—which Japan had occupied exclusively, and had fortified in absolute violation of her written word.

These islands, hundreds of them, appear only as small dots on most maps. But they cover a large strategic area. Guam lies in the middle of them—a lone outpost which we never fortified.

Under the Washington Treaty of 1921 we had solemnly agreed not to add to the fortification of the Philippine Islands. We had no safe naval base there, so we could not use the islands for extensive naval operations.

Immediately after this war started, the Japanese forces moved down on either side of the Philippines to numerous points south of them—thereby completely encircling the Islands from north, south, east and west.

It is that complete encirclement, with control of the air by Japanese land-based aircraft, which has prevented us from sending substantial reinforcements of men and material to the gallant defenders of the Philippines. For forty years it has always been our strategy—a strategy born of necessity—that in the event of a full-scale attack on the Islands by Japan, we should fight a delaying action, attempting to retire slowly into Bataan Peninsula and Corregidor.

We knew that the war as a whole would have to be fought and won by a process of attrition against Japan itself. We knew all along that, with our greater resources, we could outbuild Japan and ultimately overwhelm her on sea, on land and in the air. We knew that, to obtain our objective, many varieties of operations would be necessary in areas other than the Philippines.

Nothing that has occurred in the past two months has caused us to revise this basic strategy—except that the defense put up by General MacArthur has magnificently exceeded the previous estimates; and he and his men are gaining eternal glory therefor.

MacArthur's army of Filipinos and Americans, and the forces of the United Nations in China, in Burma and the Netherlands East Indies, are all together fulfilling the same essential task. They are making Japan pay an increasingly terrible price for her ambitious attempts to seize control of the whole Pacific world. Every Japanese transport sunk off Java is one less transport that they can use to carry reinforcements to their army opposing General MacArthur in Luzon.

It has been said that Japanese gains in the Philippines were made possible only by the success of their surprise attack on Pearl Harbor. I tell you that this is not so.

Even if the attack had not been made, your map will show that it would have been a hopeless operation for us to send the Fleet to the Philippines through thousands of miles of ocean, while all those island bases were under the sole control of the Japanese.

The consequences of the attack on Pearl Harbor—serious as they were—have been wildly exaggerated in other ways. These exaggerations come originally from Axis propagandists; but they have been repeated, I regret to say, by Americans in and out of public life.

You and I have the utmost contempt for Americans who, since Pearl Harbor, have whispered or announced "off the record" that there was no longer any Pacific Fleet—that the Fleet was all sunk or destroyed on December 7th—that more than 1,000 of our planes were destroyed on the ground. They have suggested slyly that the government has withheld the truth about casualties—that eleven or twelve thousand men were killed at Pearl Harbor instead of the figures as officially announced. They have even served the enemy propagandists by spreading the incredible story that shiploads of bodies of our honored American dead were about to arrive in New York harbor to be put in a common grave.

Almost every Axis broadcast directly quotes Americans who, by speech or in the press, make damnable misstatements such as these.

The American people realize that in many cases details of military operations cannot be disclosed until we are absolutely certain that the announcement will not give to the enemy military information which he does not already possess.

Your government has unmistakable confidence in your ability to hear the worst, without flinching or losing heart. You must, in turn, have complete confidence that your government is keeping nothing from you except information that will help the enemy in his attempt to destroy us. In a democracy there is always a solemn pact of truth between government and the people; but there must also always be a full use of discretion—and that word "discretion" applies to the critics of government as well.

This is war. The American people want to know, and will be told, the general trend of how the war is going. But they do not wish to help the enemy any more than our fighting forces do; and they will pay little attention to the rumor-mongers and poison peddlers in our midst.

To pass from the realm of rumor and poison to the field of facts: the number of our officers and men killed in the attack on Pearl Harbor on December seventh was 2,340, and the number wounded was 946. Of all the combatant ships based on Pearl Harbor—battleships, heavy cruisers, light cruisers, aircraft carriers, destroyers and submarines—only three were permanently put out of commission.

Very many of the ships of the Pacific Fleet were not even in Pearl Harbor. Some of those that were there were hit very slightly; and others that were damaged have either rejoined the Fleet by now or are still undergoing repairs. When those repairs are completed, the ships will be more efficient fighting machines than they were before.

The report that we lost more than a thousand airplanes at Pearl Harbor is as baseless as the other weird rumors. The Japanese do not know just how many planes they destroyed that day, and I am not going to tell them. But I can say that to date—and including Pearl Harbor—we have destroyed considerably more Japanese planes than they have destroyed of ours.

We have most certainly suffered losses—from Hitler's U-boats in the Atlantic as well as from the Japanese in the Pacific—and we shall suffer more of them before the turn of the tide. But, speaking for the United States of America, let me say once and for all to the people of the world: We Americans have been compelled to yield ground, but we will regain it. We and the other United Nations are committed to the destruction of the militarism of Japan and Germany. We are daily increasing our strength. Soon we, and not our enemies, will have the offensive; we, not they, will win the final battles; and we, not they, will make the final peace.

Conquered nations in Europe know what the yoke of the Nazis is like. And the people of Korea and of Manchuria know in their flesh the harsh despotism of Japan. All of the people of Asia know that if there is to be an honorable and decent future for any of them or for us, that future depends on victory by the United Nations over the forces of Axis enslavement.

If a just and durable peace is to be attained, or even if all of us are merely to save our own skins, there is one thought for us here at home to keep uppermost—the fulfillment of our special task of production—uninterrupted production. I stress that word uninterrupted.

Germany, Italy and Japan are very close to their maximum output of planes, guns, tanks and ships. The United Nations are not—especially the United States of America.

Our first job then is to build up production so that the United Nations can maintain control of the seas and attain control of the air—not merely a slight superiority, but an overwhelming superiority.

On January sixth of this year, I set certain definite goals of production for airplanes, tanks, guns and ships. The Axis propagandists called them fantastic. Tonight, nearly two months later, and after a careful survey of progress by Donald Nelson and others charged with responsibility for our production, I can tell you that those goals will be attained.

In every part of the country, experts in production and the men and women at work in the plants are giving loyal service. With few exceptions, labor, capital and farming realize that this is no time either to make undue profits or to gain special advantages, one over the other.

We are calling for new plants and additions to old plants and for plant conversion to war needs. We are seeking more men and more women to run them. We are working longer hours. We are coming to realize that one extra plane or extra tank or extra gun or extra ship completed tomorrow may, in a few months, turn the tide on some distant battlefield; it may make the difference between life and death for some of our fighting men. We know now that if we lose this war it will be generations or even centuries before our conception of democracy can live again. And we can lose this war only if we slow up our effort or if we waste our ammunition sniping at each other.

Here are three high purposes for every American:

1. We shall not stop work for a single day. If any dispute arises we shall keep on working while the dispute is solved by mediation, conciliation or arbitration—until the war is won.

2. We shall not demand special gains or special privileges or advantages for any one group or occupation.

3. We shall give up conveniences and modify the routine of our lives if our country asks us to do so. We will do it cheerfully, remembering that the common enemy seeks to destroy every home and every freedom in every part of our land.

This generation of Americans has come to realize, with a present and personal realization, that there is something larger and more important than the life of any individual or of any individual group —something for which a man will sacrifice, and gladly sacrifice, not only his pleasures, not only his goods, not only his associations with those he loves, but his life itself. In time of crisis when the future is in the balance, we come to understand, with full recognition and devotion, what this nation is, and what we owe to it.

The Axis propagandists have tried in various evil ways to destroy our determination and our morale. Failing in that, they are now trying to destroy our confidence in our own allies. They say that the British are finished—that the Russians and the Chinese are about to quit. Patriotic and sensible Americans will reject these absurdities. And instead of listening to any of this crude propaganda, they will recall some of the things that Nazis and Japanese have said and are still saying about us.

Ever since this nation became the arsenal of democracy—ever since enactment of Lend-Lease—there has been one persistent theme through all Axis propaganda.

This theme has been that Americans are admittedly rich, and that Americans have considerable industrial power—but that Americans are soft and decadent, that they cannot and will not unite and work and fight.

From Berlin, Rome and Tokyo we have been described as a nation of weaklings—"playboys"—who would hire British soldiers, or Russian soldiers, or Chinese soldiers to do our fighting for us.

Let them repeat that now!

Let them tell that to General MacArthur and his men.

Let them tell that to the sailors who today are hitting hard in the far waters of the Pacific.

Let them tell that to the boys in the Flying Fortresses.

Let them tell that to the Marines!

The United Nations constitute an association of independent peoples of equal dignity and importance. The United Nations are dedicated to a common cause. We share equally and with equal zeal the anguish and awful sacrifices of war. In the partnership of our common enterprise, we must share in a unified plan in which all of us must play our several parts, each of us being equally indispensable and dependent one on the other.

We have unified command and cooperation and comradeship.

We Americans will contribute unified production and unified acceptance of sacrifice and of effort. That means a national unity that can know no limitations of race or creed or selfish politics. The American people expect that much from themselves. And the American people will find ways and means of expressing their determination to their enemies, including the Japanese Admiral who has said that he will dictate the terms of peace here in the White House.

We of the United Nations are agreed on certain broad principles in the kind of peace we seek. The Atlantic Charter applies not only to the parts of the world that border the Atlantic but to the whole world; disarmament of aggressors, self-determination of nations and peoples, and the four freedoms—freedom of speech, freedom of religion, freedom from want, and freedom from fear.

The British and the Russian people have known the full fury of Nazi onslaught. There have been times when the fate of London and Moscow was in serious doubt. But there was never the slightest question that either the British or the Russians would yield. And today all the United Nations salute the superb Russian Army as it celebrates the twenty-fourth anniversary of its first assembly.

Though their homeland was overrun, the Dutch people are still fighting stubbornly and powerfully overseas.

The great Chinese people have suffered grievous losses; Chungking has been almost wiped out of existence—yet it remains the capital of an unbeatable China.

That is the conquering spirit which prevails throughout the United Nations in this war.

The task that we Americans now face will test us to the uttermost.

Never before have we been called upon for such a prodigious effort. Never before have we had so little time in which to do so much.

"These are the times that try men's souls."

Tom Paine wrote those words on a drum-head, by the light of a campfire. That was when Washington's little army of ragged, rugged men was retreating across New Jersey, having tasted nothing but defeat.

And General Washington ordered that these great words written by Tom Paine be read to the men of every regiment in the Continental Army, and this was the assurance given to the first American armed forces:

"The summer soldier and the sunshine patriot will, in this crisis, shrink from the service of their country; but he that stands it now, deserves the love and thanks of man and woman. Tyranny, like hell, is not easily conquered; yet we have this consolation with us, that the harder the sacrifice, the more glorious the triumph."

So spoke Americans in the year 1776.

So speak Americans today!

FLAG DAY ADDRESS

June 13, 1942

Today on Flag Day we celebrate the declaration of the United Nations—that great alliance dedicated to the defeat of our foes and to the establishment of a true peace based on the freedom of man. Today the Republic of Mexico and the Commonwealth of the Philippine Islands join us. We welcome these valiant peoples to the company of those who fight for freedom.

The four freedoms of common humanity are as much elements of man's needs as air and sunlight, bread and salt. Deprive him of a part of these freedoms and he dies—deprive him of a part of them and a part of him withers. Give them to him in full and abundant measure and he will cross the threshhold of a new age, the greatest age of man.

These freedoms are the rights of men of every creed and every race, wherever they live. This is their heritage, long withheld. We of the United Nations have the power and the men and the will at last to assure man's heritage.

The belief in the four freedoms of common humanity—the belief in man, created free, in the image of God—is the crucial difference between ourselves and the enemies we face today. In it lies the absolute unity of our alliance, opposed to the oneness of the evil we hate. Here is our heritage, the source and promise of victory.

We of the United Nations know that our faith cannot be broken by any man or any force. And we know that there are other millions who in their silent captivity share our belief.

We ask the German people, still dominated by their Nazi whipmasters, whether they would rather have the mechanized hell of Hitler's "New" Order or—in place of that—freedom of speech and religion, freedom from want and from fear.

We ask the Japanese people, trampled by their savage lords of slaughter, whether they would rather continue slavery and blood or, in place of them—freedom of speech and religion, freedom from want and fear.

We ask the brave, unconquered people of the nations the Axis invaders have dishonored and despoiled whether they would rather yield to conquerors or—have freedom of speech and religion, freedom from want and from fear.

We know the answer. They know the answer. We know that man, born to freedom in the image of God, will not forever suffer the oppressors' sword. The peoples of the United Nations are taking that sword from the oppressors' hands. With it they will destroy those tyrants. The brazen tyrannies pass. Man marches forward toward the light.

I am going to close by reading you a prayer that has been written for the United Nations on this Day:

"God of the free, we pledge our hearts and lives today to the cause of all free mankind.

"Grant us victory over the tyrants who would enslave all free men and nations. Grant us faith and understanding to cherish all those who fight for freedom as if they were our brothers. Grant us brotherhood in hope and union, not only for the space of this bitter war, but for the days to come which shall and must unite all the children of earth.

"Our earth is but a small star in the great universe. Yet of it we can make, if we choose, a planet unvexed by war, untroubled by hunger or fear, undivided by senseless distinctions of race, color or theory. Grant us that courage and foreseeing to begin this task today that our children and our children's children may be proud of the name of man.

"The spirit of man has awakened and the soul of man has gone forth. Grant us the wisdom and the vision to comprehend the greatness of man's spirit, that suffers and endures so hugely for a goal beyond his own brief span. Grant us honor for our dead who died in the faith, honor for our living who work and strive for the faith, redemption and security for all captive lands and peoples. Grant us patience with the deluded and pity for the betrayed. And grant us the skill and the valor that shall cleanse the world of oppression and the old base doctrine that the strong must eat the weak because they are strong.

"Yet most of all grant us brotherhood, not only for this day but for all our years—a brotherhood not of words but of acts and deeds. We are all of us children of earth—grant us that simple knowledge. If our brothers are oppressed, then we are oppressed. If they hunger, we hunger. If their freedom is taken away, our freedom is not secure. Grant us a common faith that man shall know bread and peace—that he shall know justice and righteousness, freedom and security, an equal opportunity and an equal chance to do his best, not only in our own lands, but throughout the world. And in that faith let us march toward the clean world our hand can make. Amen."

NEW DEAL SPEECH BEFORE THE DEMOCRATIC NATIONAL CONVENTION

July 2, 1932

I appreciate your willingness after these six arduous days to remain here, for I know well the sleepless hours which you and I have had. I regret that I am late, but I have no control over the winds of Heaven and could only be thankful for my Navy training.

The appearance before a National Convention of its nominee for President, to be formally notified of his selection, is unprecedented and unusual, but these are unprecedented and unusual times. I have started out on the tasks that lie ahead by breaking the absurd traditions that the candidate should remain in professed ignorance of what has happened for weeks until he is formally notified of that event many weeks later.

My friends, may this be the symbol of my intention to be honest and to avoid all hypocrisy or sham, to avoid all silly shutting of the eyes to the truth in this campaign. You have nominated me and I know it, and I am here to thank you for the honor.

Let it also be symbolic that in so doing I broke traditions. Let it be from now on the task of our Party to break foolish traditions. We will break foolish traditions and leave it to the Republican leadership, far more skilled in that art, to break promises.

Let us now and here highly resolve to resume the country's interrupted march along the path of real progress, of real justice, of real equality for all of our citizens, great and small. Our indomitable leader in that interrupted march is no longer with us, but there still survives today his spirit. Many of his captains, thank God, are still with us, to give us wise counsel. Let us feel that in everything we do there still lives with us, if not the body, the great indomitable, unquenchable, progressive soul of our Commander-in-Chief, Woodrow Wilson.

I have many things on which I want to make my position clear at the earliest possible moment in this campaign. That admirable document, the platform which you have adopted, is clear. I accept it one hundred per cent.

And you can accept my pledge that I will leave no doubt or ambiguity on where I stand on any question of moment in this campaign.

As we enter this new battle, let us keep always present with us some of the ideals of the Party: The fact that the Democratic Party by tradition and by the continuing logic of history, past and present, is the bearer of liberalism and of progress and at the same time of safety to our institutions. And if this appeal fails, remember well, my friends, that a resentment against the failure of Republican leadership—and note well that in this campaign I shall not use the words "Republican Party," but I shall use, day in and day out, the words, "Republican leadership"—the failure of Republican leaders to solve our troubles may degenerate into unreasoning radicalism.

The great social phenomenon of this depression, unlike others before it, is that it has produced but a few of the disorderly manifestations that too often attend upon such times.

Wild radicalism has made few converts, and the greatest tribute that I can pay to my countrymen is that in these days of crushing want there persists an orderly and hopeful spirit on the part of the millions of our people who have suffered so much. To fail to offer them a new chance is not only to betray their hopes but to misunderstand their patience.

To meet by reaction that danger of radicalism is to invite disaster. Reaction is no barrier to the radical. It is a challenge, a provocation. The way to meet that danger is to offer a workable program of reconstruction, and the party to offer it is the party with clean hands.

This, and this only, is a proper protection against blind reaction on the one hand and an improvised, hit-or-miss, irresponsible opportunism on the other.

There are two ways of viewing the Government's duty in matters affecting economic and social life. The first sees to it that a favored few are helped and hopes that some of their prosperity will leak through, sift through, to labor, to the farmer, to the small business man. That theory belongs to the party of Toryism, and I had hoped that most of the Tories left this country in 1776.

But it is not and never will be the theory of the Democratic Party. This is no time for fear, for reaction or for timidity. Here and now I invite those nominal Republicans who find that their conscience cannot be squared with the groping and the failure of their party leaders to join hands with us; here and now, in equal measure, I warn those nominal Democrats who squint at the future with their faces turned toward the past, and who feel no responsibility to the demands of the new time, that they are out of step with their Party.

Yes, the people of this country want a genuine choice this year, not a choice between two names for the same reactionary doctrine. Ours must be a party of liberal thought, of planned action, of enlightened international outlook, and of the greatest good to the greatest number of our citizens.

Now it is inevitable—and the choice is that of the times—it is inevitable that the main issue of this campaign should revolve about the clear fact of our economic condition, a depression so deep that it is without precedent in modern history. It will not do merely to state, as do Republican leaders to explain their broken promises of continued inaction, that the depression is worldwide. That was not their explanation of the apparent prosperity of 1928. The people will not forget the claim made by them then that prosperity was only a domestic product manufactured by a Republican President and a Republican Congress. If they claim paternity for the one they cannot deny paternity for the other.

I cannot take up all the problems today. I want to touch on a few that are vital. Let us look a little at the recent history and the simple economics, the kind of economics that you and I and the average man and woman talk.

In the years before 1929 we know that this country had completed a vast cycle of building and inflation; for ten years we expanded on the theory of repairing the wastes of the War, but actually expanding far beyond that, and also beyond our natural and normal growth. Now it is worth remembering, and the cold figures of finance prove it, that during that time there was little or no drop in the prices that the consumer had to pay, although those same figures proved that the cost of production fell very greatly; corporate profit resulting from this period was enormous; at the same time little of that profit was devoted to the reduction of prices. The consumer was forgotten. Very little of it went into increased wages; the worker was forgotten, and by no means an adequate proportion was even paid out in dividends—the stockholder was forgotten.

And, incidentally, very little of it was taken by taxation to the beneficent Government of those years.

What was the result? Enormous corporate surpluses piled up —the most stupendous in history. Where, under the spell of delirious speculation, did those surpluses go? Let us talk economics that the figures prove and that we can understand. Why, they went chiefly in two directions: first, into new and unnecessary plants which now stand stark and idle; and second, into the call-money market of Wall Street, either directly by the corporations, or indirectly through the banks. Those are the facts. Why blink at them?

Then came the crash. You know the story. Surpluses invested in unnecessary plants became idle. Men lost their jobs; purchasing power dried up; banks became frightened and started calling loans. Those who had money were afraid to part with it. Credit contracted. Industry stopped. Commerce declined, and unemployment mounted.

And there we are today.

Translate that into human terms. See how the events of the past three years have come home to specific groups of people: first, the group dependent on industry; second, the group dependent on agriculture; third, and made up in large part of members of the first two groups, the people who are called "small investors and depositors." In fact, the strongest possible tie between the first two groups, agriculture and industry, is the fact that the savings and to a degree the security of both are tied together in that third group—the credit structure of the Nation.

Never in history have the interests of all the people been so united in a single economic problem. Picture to yourself, for instance, the great groups of property owned by millions of our citizens, represented by credits issued in the form of bonds and mortgages—Government bonds of all kinds, Federal, State, county, municipal; bonds of industrial companies, of utility companies; mortgages on real estate in farms and cities, and finally the vast investments of the Nation in the railroads. What is the measure of the security of each of those groups? We know well that in our complicated, interrelated credit structure if any one of these credit groups collapses they may all collapse. Danger to one is danger to all.

How, I ask, has the present Administration in Washington treated the interrelationship of these credit groups? The answer is clear: It has not recognized that interrelationship existed at all. Why, the Nation asks, has Washington failed to understand that all of these groups, each and every one, the top of the pyramid and the bottom of the pyramid, must be considered together, that each and every one of them is dependent on every other; each and every one of them affecting the whole financial fabric?

Statesmanship and vision, my friends, require relief to all at the same time.

Just one word or two on taxes, the taxes that all of us pay toward the cost of Government of all kinds.

I know something of taxes. For three long years I have been going up and down this country preaching that Government—Federal and State and local—costs too much. I shall not stop that preaching. As an immediate program of action we must abolish useless offices. We must eliminate unnecessary functions of Government—functions, in fact, that are not definitely essential to the continuance of Government. We must merge, we must consolidate subdivisions of Government, and, like the private citizen, give up luxuries which we can no longer afford.

By our example at Washington itself, we shall have the opportunity of pointing the way of economy to local government, for let us remember well that out of every tax dollar in the average State in this Nation, forty cents enter the treasury in Washington, D. C., ten or twelve cents only go to the State capitals, and forty-eight cents are consumed by the costs of local government in counties and cities and towns.

I propose to you, my friends, and through you, that Government of all kinds, big and little, be made solvent and that the example be set by the President of the United States and his Cabinet.

And talking about setting a definite example, I congratulate this convention for having had the courage fearlessly to write into its declaration of principles what an overwhelming majority here assembled really thinks about the Eighteenth Amendment. This convention wants repeal. Your candidate wants repeal. And I am confident that the United States of America wants repeal.

Two years ago the platform on which I ran for Governor the second time contained substantially the same provision. The overwhelming sentiment of the people of my State, as shown by the vote of that year, extends, I know, to the people of many of the other states. I say to you now that from this date on the Eighteenth Amendment is doomed. When that happens, we as Democrats must and will, rightly and morally, enable the States to protect themselves against the importation of intoxicating liquor where such importation may violate their State laws. We must, rightly and morally, prevent the return of the saloon.

To go back to this dry subject of finance, because it all ties in together—the Eighteenth Amendment has something to do with finance, too—in a comprehensive planning for the reconstruction of the great credit groups, including Government credit, I list an important place for that prize statement of principle in the platform here adopted calling for the letting in of the light of day on issues of securities, foreign and domestic, which are offered for sale to the investing public.

My friends, you and I as common-sense citizens know that it would help to protect the savings of the country from the dishonesty of crooks and from the lack of honor of some men in high financial places. Publicity is the enemy of crookedness.

And now one word about unemployment, and incidentally about agriculture. I have favored the use of certain types of public works as a further emergency means of stimulating employment and the issuance of bonds to pay for such public works, but I have pointed out that no economic end is served if we merely build without building for a necessary purpose. Such works, of course, should insofar as possible be self-sustaining if they are to be financed by the issuing of bonds. So as to spread the points of all kinds as widely as possible, we must take definite steps to shorten the working day and the working week.

Let us use common sense and business sense. Just as one example, we know that a very hopeful and immediate means of relief, both for the unemployed and for agriculture, will come from a wide plan of the converting of many millions of acres of marginal and unused land into timberland through reforestation. There are tens of millions of acres east of the Mississippi River alone in abandoned farms, in cut-over land, now growing up in worthless brush. Why, every European Nation has a definite land policy, and has had one for generations. We have none. Having none, we face a future of soil erosion and timber famine. It is clear that economic foresight and immediate employment march hand in hand in the call for the reforestation of these vast areas.

In so doing, employment can be given to a million men. That is the kind of public work that is self-sustaining, and therefore capable of being financed by the issuance of bonds which are made secure by the fact that the growth of tremendous crops will provide adequate security for the investment.

Yes, I have a very definite program for providing employment by that means. I have done it, and I am doing it today in the State of New York. I know that the Democratic Party can do it successfully in the Nation. That will put men to work, and that is an example of the action that we are going to have.

Now as a further aid to agriculture, we know perfectly well —but have we come out and said so clearly and distinctly—we should repeal immediately those provisions of law that compel the Federal Government to go into the market to purchase, to sell, to speculate in farm products in a futile attempt to reduce farm surpluses. And they are the people who are talking of keeping Government out of business. The practical way to help the farmer is by an arrangement that will, in addition to lightening some of the impoverishing burdens from his back, do something toward the reduction of the surpluses of staple commodities that hang on the market. It should be our aim to add to the world prices of staple products the amount of a reasonable tariff protection, to give agriculture the same protection that industry has today.

And in exchange for this immediately increased return I am sure that the farmers of this Nation would agree ultimately to such planning of their production as would reduce the surpluses and make it unnecessary in later years to depend on dumping those surpluses abroad in order to support domestic prices. That result has been accomplished in other Nations; why not in America, too?

Farm leaders and farm economists, generally, agree that a plan based on that principle is a desirable first step in the reconstruction of agriculture. It does not in itself furnish a complete program, but it will serve in great measure in the long run to remove the pall of a surplus without the continued perpetual threat of world dumping. Final voluntary reduction of surplus is a part of our objective, but the long continuance and the present burden of existing surpluses make it necessary to repair great damage of the present by immediate emergency measures.

Such a plan as that, my friends, does not cost the Government any money, nor does it keep the Government in business or in speculation.

As to the actual wording of a bill, I believe that the Democratic Party stands ready to be guided by whatever the responsible farm groups themselves agree on. That is a principle that is sound; and again I ask for action.

One more word about the farmer, and I know that every delegate in this hall who lives in the city knows why I lay emphasis on the farmer. It is because one-half of our population, over fifty million people, are dependent on agriculture; and, my friends, if those fifty million people have no money, no cash, to buy what is produced in the city, the city suffers to an equal or greater extent.

That is why we are going to make the voters understand this year that this Nation is not merely a Nation of independence, but it is, if we are to survive, bound to be a Nation of interdependence —town and city, and North and South, East and West. That is our goal, and that goal will be understood by the people of this country no matter where they live.

Yes, the purchasing power of that half of our population dependent on agriculture is gone. Farm mortgages reach nearly ten billions of dollars today and interest charges on that alone are five hundred sixty million dollars a year. But that is not all. The tax burden caused by extravagant and inefficient local government is an additional factor. Our most immediate concern should be to reduce the interest burden on these mortgages.

Rediscounting of farm mortgages under salutary restrictions must be expanded and should, in the future, be conditioned on the reduction of interest rates. Amortization payments, maturities should likewise in this crisis be extended before rediscount is permitted where the mortgagor is sorely pressed. That my friends, is another example of practical, immediate relief: Action.

I aim to do the same thing, and it can be done, for the small home-owner in our cities and villages. We can lighten his burden and develop his purchasing power. Take away, my friends, that spectre of too high an interest rate. Take away that spectre of the due date just a short time away. Save homes; save homes for thousands of self-respecting families, and drive out that spectre of insecurity from our midst.

Out of all the tons of printed paper, out of all the hours of oratory, the recriminations, the defenses, the happy-thought plans in Washington and in every State, there emerges one great, simple, crystal-pure fact that during the past ten years a Nation of one hundred twenty million people has been led by the Republican leaders to erect an impregnable barbed wire entanglement around its borders through the instrumentality of tariffs which have isolated us from all the other human beings in all the rest of the round world. I accept that admirable tariff statement in the platform of this convention. It would protect American business and American labor. By our acts of the past we have invited and received the retaliation of other nations. I propose an invitation to them to forget the past, to sit at the table wtih us, as friends, and to plan with us for the restoration of the trade of the world.

Go into the home of the business man. He knows what the tariff has done for him. Go into the home of the factory worker. He knows why goods do not move. Go into the home of the farmer. He knows how the tariff has helped to ruin him.

At last our eyes are open. At last the American people are ready to acknowledge that Republican leadership was wrong and that the Democracy is right.

My program, of which I can only touch on these points, is based upon this simple moral principle: the welfare and the soundness of a nation depend first upon what the great mass of the people wish and need; and second, whether or not they are getting it.

What do the people of America want more than anything else? To my mind, they want two things: work, with all the moral and spiritual values that go with it; and with work, a reasonable measure of security—security for themselves and for their wives and children. Work and security—these are more than words. They are more than facts. They are the spiritual values, the true goal toward which our efforts of reconstruction should lead. These are the values that this program is intended to gain; these are the values we have failed to achieve by the leadership we now have.

Our Republican leaders tell us economic laws—sacred, inviolable, unchangeable—cause panics which no one could prevent. But while they prate of economic laws, men and women are starving. We must lay hold of the fact that economic laws are not made by nature. They are made by human beings.

Yes, when—not if—when we get the chance, the Federal Government will assume bold leadership in distress relief. For years Washington has alternated between putting its head in the sand and saying there is no large number of destitute people in our midst who need food and clothing, and then saying the States should take care of them, if there are. Instead of planning two and a half years ago to do what they are now trying to do, they kept putting it off from day to day, week to week, and month to month, until the conscience of America demanded action.

I say that while primary responsibility for relief rests with localities now, as ever, yet the Federal Government has always had and still has a continuing responsibility for the broader public welfare. It will soon fulfill that responsibility.

And now, just a few words about our plans for the next four months. By coming here instead of waiting for a formal notification, I have made it clear that I believe we should eliminate expensive ceremonies and that we should set in motion at once, tonight my friends, the necessary machinery for an adequate presentation of the issues to the electorate of the Nation.

I myself have important duties as Governor of a great State, duties which in these times are more arduous and more grave than at any previous period. Yet I feel confident that I shall be able to make a number of short visits to several parts of the Nation. My trips will have as their first objective the study at first hand, from the lips of men and women of all parties and all occupations, of the actual conditions and needs of every part of an interdependent country.

One word more: Out of every crisis, every tribulation, every disaster, mankind rises with some share of greater knowledge, of higher decency, of purer purpose. Today we shall have come through a period of loose thinking, descending morals, an era of selfishness, among individual men and women and among nations. Blame not Governments alone for this. Blame ourselves in equal share. Let us be frank in acknowledgment of the truth that many amongst us have made obeisance to Mammon, that the profits of speculation, the easy road without toil, have lured us from the old barricades. To return to higher standards we must abandon the false prophets and seek new leaders of our own choosing.

Never before in modern history have the essential differences between the two major American parties stood out in such striking contrast as they do today. Republican leaders not only have failed in material things, they have failed in national vision, because in disaster they have held out no hope, they have pointed out no path for the people below to climb back to places of security and of safety in our American life.

Throughout the Nation, men and women, forgotten in the political philosophy of the Government of the last years look to us here for guidance and for more equitable opportunity to share in the distribution of national wealth.

On the farms, in the large metropolitan areas, in the smaller cities and in the villages, millions of our citizens cherish the hope that their old standards of living and of thought have not gone forever. Those millions cannot and shall not hope in vain.

I pledge you, I pledge myself, to a new deal for the American people. Let us all here assembled constitute ourselves prophets of a new order of competence and of courage. This is more than a political campaign; it is a call to arms. Give me your help, not to win votes alone, but to win in this crusade to restore America to its own people.

WAR MESSAGE TO CONGRESS

December 8, 1941

Yesterday, December 7, 1941—a date which will live in infamy —the United States of America was suddenly and deliberately attacked by naval and air forces of the Empire of Japan.

The United States was at peace with that nation and, at the solicitation of Japan, was still in conversation with its government and its Emperor looking toward the maintenance of peace in the Pacific. Indeed, one hour after Japanese air squadrons had commenced bombing in Oahu, the Japanese ambassador to the United States and his colleague delivered to the Secretary of State a formal reply to a recent American message. While this reply stated that it seemed useless to continue the existing diplomatic negotiations, it contained no threat or hint of war or armed attack.

It will be recorded that the distance of Hawaii from Japan makes it obvious that the attack was deliberately planned many days or even weeks ago. During the intervening time the Japanese Government has deliberately sought to deceive the United States by false statements and expressions of hope for continued peace.

The attack yesterday on the Hawaiian Islands has caused severe damage to American naval and military forces. Very many American lives have been lost. In addition American ships have been reported torpedoed on the high seas between San Francisco and Honolulu.

Yesterday the Japanese government also launched an attack against Malaya.

Last night Japanese forces attacked Hong Kong.
Last night Japanese forces attacked Guam.
Last night Japanese forces attacked the Philippine Islands.
Last night the Japanese attacked Wake Island.

This morning the Japanese attacked Midway Island.

Japan has, therefore, undertaken a surprise offensive extending throughout the Pacific area. The facts of yesterday speak for themselves. The people of the United States have already formed their opinions and well understand the implications to the very life and safety of our nation.

As Commander-in-Chief of the Army and Navy, I have directed that all measures be taken for our defense.

Always will we remember the character of the onslaught against us.

No matter how long it may take us to overcome this premeditated invasion, the American people in their righteous might will win through to absolute victory.

I believe I interpret the will of the Congress and of the people when I assert that we will not only defend ourselves to the uttermost but will make very certain that this form of treachery shall never endanger us again.

Hostilities exist. There is no blinking at the fact that our people, our territory and our interests are in grave danger.

With confidence in our armed forces—with the unbounding determination of our people—we will gain the inevitable triumph —so help us God.

I ask that the Congress declare that since the unprovoked and dastardly attack by Japan on Sunday, December 7th, a state of war has existed between the United States and the Japanese Empire.

RESPONSE TO ADDRESS BY PRESIDENT AVILA CAMACHO
April 20, 1943

Senor Presidente, La Republica Mexicana.

My friends and good neighbors.

Your Excellency's friendly and cordial expressions add to the very great pleasure which I feel at being here on Mexican soil.

It is an amazing thing to have to realize that nearly thirty-four years have passed since the Chief Executives of our two countries have met face to face. I hope in the days to come every Mexican and every American President will feel at liberty to visit each other just as neighbors visit each other—just as neighbors talk things over and get to know each other better.

Our two countries owe their independence to the fact that your ancestors and mine held the same truths to be worth fighting for and dying for. Hidalgo and Juarez were men of the same stamp as Washington and Jefferson. It was, therefore, inevitable that our two countries should find themselves aligned together in the great struggle which is being fought today to determine whether this shall be a free or a slave world.

The attacks of the Axis powers during the past few years against our common heritage as free men culminated in the unspeakable and unprovoked aggression of Dec. 7, 1941, and of May 14, 1942, and the shedding of blood on those dates of citizens of the United States and of Mexico alike.

Those attacks did not find the Western Hemisphere unprepared. The twenty-one free republics of the Americas during the past ten years have devised a system of international cooperation which has become a great bulwark in the defense of our heritage and the defense of our future. That system, whose strength is now evident even to the most skeptical, is based primarily upon the renunciation of the use of force and is based on the enshrining of international justice and mutual respect as the governing rule of conduct by all nations.

In the forging of that new international policy the role of Mexico has been outstanding. Mexican Presidents and Foreign Ministers have appreciated the nature of the struggle with which we are now confronted at a time when many other nations much closer to the focus of infection were blind.

The wisdom of the measures which the statesmen of Mexico and the United States, and of the other American Republics have adopted at inter-American gatherings during recent years has been amply demonstrated. They have succeeded because they have been placed in effect not only in Mexico and the United States but by all except one of the other American republics.

You and I, Mr. President, are Commanders-in-Chief of our respective armed forces, and we have been able to concert measures for common defense. The harmony and mutual confidence which has prevailed between our armies and navies is beyond praise. Brotherhood in arms has been established.

The determination of the Mexican people and of their leaders has led to production on an all-out basis of strategic and vital materials so necessary to the forging of the weapons destined to compass the final overthrow of our common foe. In this great city of Monterey, I have been most impressed with the singleminded purpose with which all the forces of production are joined together in the war effort.

And, too, Mexican farm workers, brought to the United States in accordance with an agreement between our two governments, the terms of which are fully consonant with the social objectives that we cherish together, are contributing their skill and toil to the production of vitally needed food.

But not less important than the military cooperation and the production of supplies needed for the maintenance of our respective economies has been the exchange of those ideas and those moral values which give life and significance to the tremendous effort of the free peoples of the world. We in the United States have listened with admiration and with profit to your statements and addresses, Mr. President, and to those of your distinguished Foreign Minister. We have gained inspiration and strength from your words.

In the shaping of a common victory our peoples are finding that they have common aspirations. They can work together for a common objective. Let us never lose our hold upon that truth. It contains within it the secret of future happiness and prosperity for all of us on both sides of our unfortified border.

Let us make sure that when our victory is won, when the forces of evil surrender—and that surrender shall be unconditional—then we, with the same spirit and with the same united courage, will face the task of the building for a better world.

There is much work still to be done by men of good-will on both sides of the border. The great Mexican people have their feet set upon a path of ever greater progress so that each nation may enjoy the greatest possible measure of security and opportunity. The Government of the United States and my countrymen are ready to help to that progress.

We recognize a mutual interdependence of our joint resources. We know that Mexico's resources will be developed for the common good of humanity. And we know that the day of the exploitation of the resources and the people of one country for the benefit of any group in another country is definitely over.

It is time that every citizen in every one of the American republics recognizes that the Good Neighbor policy means that harm to one republic means harm to each and every one of the other republics. We have all of us recognized the principle of independence. It is time that we recognize also the privilege of interdependence—one upon another.

Mr. President, it is my hope that in the expansion of our common effort in this war and in the peace to follow we will again have occasion for friendly consultation in order further to promote the closest understanding and continued unity of purpose between our two peoples.

We have achieved close understanding and unity of purpose and I am grateful to you, Mr. President, and to the Mexican people for this opportunity to meet you on Mexican soil and to call you friends.

You and I are breaking another precedent. Let these meetings between the President of Mexico and the United States recur again and again and again.

FOURTH INAUGURAL ADDRESS

January 20, 1945

You will understand and, I believe, agree with my wish that the form of this inauguration be simple and its words brief.

We Americans of today, together with our Allies, are passing through a period of supreme test. It is a test of our courage—of our resolve—of our wisdom—of our essential decency.

If we meet that test—successfully and honorably—we shall perform a service of historic importance which men and women and children will honor throughout all time.

As I stand here today, having taken the solemn oath of office in the presence of my fellow countrymen—in the presence of our God—I know that it is America's purpose that we shall not fail.

In the days and in the years that are to come we shall work for a just and durable peace as today we work and fight for total victory in war.

We can and we will achieve such a peace.

We shall strive for perfection. We shall not achieve it immediately—but we still shall strive. We may make mistakes—but they must never be mistakes which result from faintness of heart or abandonment of moral principle.

I remember that my old schoolmaster said, in days that seemed to us then to be secure and untroubled: "Things in life will not always run smoothly. Sometimes we will be rising toward the heights—then all will seem to reverse itself and start downward. The great fact to remember is that the trend of civilization itself is forever upward; that a line drawn through the middle of the peaks and valleys of the centuries always has an upward trend."

Our Constitution of 1787 was not a perfect instrument; it is not perfect yet. But it provided a firm base on which all manner of men, of all races and colors and creeds, could build our solid structure of democracy.

Today in this year of war, 1945, we have learned lessons—at a fearful cost—and we shall profit by them.

We have learned that we cannot live alone, at peace; that our own well-being is dependent on the well-being of other nations —far away. We have learned that we must live as men, not as ostriches, nor as dogs in the manger.

We have learned to be citizens of the world, members of the human community.

We have learned the simple truth.

Emerson said, that "the only way to have a friend is to be one."

We can gain no lasting peace if we approach it with suspicion and mistrust—and with fear. We can gain it only if we proceed with the understanding and confidence and courage which flow from conviction.

The Almighty God has blessed our land in many ways. He has given our people stout hearts and strong arms with which to strike mighty blows for freedom and truth. He has given to our country a faith which has become the hope of all peoples in an anguished world.

We pray now to Him for the vision to see our way clearly—to see the way that leads to a better life for ourselves and for all our fellow men—to the achievement of His will to peace on earth.

UNDELIVERED ADDRESS

April 13, 1945

ATLANTA, April 13, 1945 (*AP*)—*The late President Roosevelt, in a speech written the night before he died, declared that Americans were determined there should not be a Third World War.*

The text of the speech, which he was to have delivered by radio tonight in observance of 350 Jefferson Day dinners throughout the country, was handed to reporters by Presidential Secretary Stephen Early as the funeral train paused at the railroad terminal here. The dinners have been canceled.

Mr. Early said that Mr. Roosevelt would have delivered the address without disclosing that he was in Warm Springs.

The text follows:

Americans are gathered together this evening in communities all over the country to pay tribute to the living memory of Thomas Jefferson—one of the greatest of all democrats; and I want to make it clear that I am spelling that word "democrats" with a small "d."

I wish I had the power, just for this evening, to be present at all of these gatherings.

In this historic year, more than ever before, we do well to consider the character of Thomas Jefferson as an American citizen of the world.

As Minister to France, then as our first Secretary of State and as our third President, Jefferson was instrumental in the establishment of the United States as a vital factor in international affairs.

It was he who first sent our Navy into far distant waters to defend our rights. And the promulgation of the Monroe Doctrine was the logical development of Jefferson's far-seeing foreign policy.

Today, this nation which Jefferson helped so greatly to build, is playing a tremendous part in the battle for the rights of man all over the world.

Today we are part of the vast allied force—a force composed of flesh and blood and steel and spirit—which is today destroying the makers of war, the breeders of hate, in Europe and in Asia.

In Jefferson's time our Navy consisted of only a handful of frigates—but that tiny Navy taught nations across the Atlantic that piracy in the Mediterranean—acts of aggression against peaceful commerce, and the enslavement of their crews, was one of those things which, among neighbors, simply was not done.

Today, we have learned in the agony of war that great power involves great responsibility. Today, we can no more escape the consequences of German and Japanese aggression than could he avoid the consequences of attacks by the Barbary corsairs a century and a half before.

We, as Americans, do not choose to deny our responsibility.

Nor do we intend to abandon our determination that, within the lives of our children and our children's children, there will not be a Third World War.

We seek peace—enduring peace. More than an end to war, we want an end to the beginnings of all wars—yes, an end to this brutal, inhuman and thoroughly impractical method of settling the differences between governments.

The once powerful, malignant Nazi state is crumbling, the Japanese war lords are receiving, in their own homeland, the retribution for which they asked when they attacked Pearl Harbor.

But the mere conquest of our enemies is not enough.

We must go on to do all in our power to conquer the doubts and the fears, the ignorance and the greed, which made this horror possible.

Thomas Jefferson, himself a distinguished scientist, once spoke of the "brotherly spirit of science, which unites into one family all its votaries of whatever grade, and however widely dispersed throughout the different quarters of the globe."

Today science has brought all the different quarters of the globe so close together that it is impossible to isolate them one from another.

Today we are faced with the pre-eminent fact that, if civilization is to survive, we must cultivate the science of human relationships—the ability of all peoples, of all kinds, to live together and work together, in the same world, at peace.

Let me assure you that my hand is the steadier for the work that is to be done, that I move more firmly into the task, knowing that you—millions and millions of you—are joined with me in the resolve to make this work endure.

The work, my friends, is peace, more than an end of this war —an end to the beginnings of all wars, yes, an end, forever, to this impractical, unrealistic settlement of the differences between governments by the mass killing of peoples.

Today as we move against the terrible scourge of war—as we go forward toward the greatest contribution that any generation of human beings can make in this world—the contribution of lasting peace, I ask you to keep up your faith. I measure the sound, solid achievement that can be made at this time by the straight-edge of your own confidence and your resolve. And to you, and to all Americans who dedicate themselves with us to the making of an abiding peace, I say:

The only limit to our realization of tomorrow will be our doubts of today. Let us move forward with strong and active faith.

CPSIA information can be obtained
at www.ICGtesting.com
Printed in the USA
BVHW060031010720
582552BV00004B/623

9 781497 969308